D0636621

Stately Ghosts

Stately**Ghosts**

Haunting tales from Britain's historic houses

Published by VisitBritain Publishing in association with the Historic Houses Asso...

VisitBritain Publishing
Thames Tower, Blacks Road, London W6 9EL

First published 2007

© British Tourist Authority (trading as VisitBritain) with Complete Editions 2007

ISBN 978-0-7095-8424-7

A CIP catalogue record for this book is available from the British Library.

The information contained in this publication has been published in good faith on the basis of information submitted to VisitBritain and is believed to be correct at time of going to press. Nevertheless, VisitBritain regrets that it cannot guarantee complete accuracy and all liability for loss, disappointment, negligence or other damages caused by reliance on the information contained in this publication, is hereby excluded.

Picture Credits: The Marsden Archive Cover, 25, 59, 80, 93, 109/ Getty Images 8/ Mary Evans 11, 42, 48, 53, 61, 62, 63, 83, 87, 89, 107/ Kiplin Hall 13, 14, 71/ Prideaux Place 16/ Owlpen Manor 17, 18, 100/ Sausmarez Manor 20, 54, 123/ Ripley Castle 23, 108/ Brian Sherwin 27, 118/ Eyam Hall 29, 100/ Tissington Hall 29, 32/ His Grace The Duke of Bedford & the Trustees of the Bedford Estate 36, 39/ Lord Montagu of Beaulieu 39, 40/ Britain on View 46, 84, Britain on View/Jill Swainson 114/ Country Life Picture Library 50, 73, 119/ The Rt Hon. The Earl of Derby/Garry Catterall 51/ Visit Scotland/Scottish Viewpoint 55, 57/ Traquair House 67, 68/ Ballindalloch Castle 75, 76, 78/ Levens Hall/Andrew Semple 88, 117/ The Marquess of Bath, Longleat House 96, 98/ Bramall Hall 101/Burton Agnes Hall 103, 105/ Heritage House Publishing/Nick McCann 115/ Powderham Castle 125

Designed and produced for VisitBritain Publishing by Susanna Geoghegan Gift Publishing Consultancy
Publishing Manager for VisitBritain, Jane Collinson
Picture research by Emma Pearce
Printed in China

HISTORIC HOUSES ASSOCIATION

Contents

Foreword

Stately Ghosts follows three books in the 'Then and Now' series, which were published in association with the Historic Houses Association (HHA) in 2006. The interest in ghosts and supernatural phenomena of all kinds attracts a growing number of visitors to Britain's historic houses and is helping to boost the contribution they make to the wider economy. With more than 15 million visitors, providing employment for upwards of 10,000 people (who annually earn in excess of £85 million) and contributing an estimated £1.6–£2 billion each year to the rural economy, our historic houses form a vital link between past and present.

Although the focus of *Stately Ghosts* is self-evidently directed at previous generations of owners and occupants, it is the help of present-day owners, curators and administrators that has made this book possible. In addition to assisting with the provision of pictures, many have made themselves available for interviews, while others have supplied a range of archive material and more than a few have put pen to paper (perhaps fingers to keyboard is more accurate – if less lyrical) and have written accounts of their ghost stories in their own words. To them all we extend our very grateful thanks, in particular the following, who have been directly involved in the evolution of the book:

At the HHA itself, Peter Sinclair, Fiona Attenborough and Clare Mahon.

At Ballindalloch Castle, Mrs Clare Macpherson-Grant Russell Laird of Ballindalloch and Fenella Corrs.

At Beaulieu, Susan Tomkins.

At Bramall Hall, Helen Jones.

At Burton Agnes Hall, Simon Cunliffe-Lister.

At Chavenage House, Caroline Lowsley-Williams and her father David Lowsley-Williams.

At Chenies Manor House, Mrs Elizabeth MacLeod-Matthews and Susan Brock.

At Chillingham Castle, Sir Humphry Wakefield Bt.

At Duncombe Park, Lord Feversham.

At Dunvegan Castle, Maureen Byers.

At Eyam Hall, Mrs Nicola Wright and Jeremy Wright.

At Glamis Castle, Charlotte Fleming.

At Iford Manor, Mrs Elizabeth Cartwright-Hignett.

At Isel Hall, Miss Mary Burkett.

At Kiplin Hall, Dawn Webster.

At Knebworth House, Henry Lytton-Cobbold and Clare Fleck.

At Knowsley Hall, The Earl of Derby, Andrea Poole and Emma Tate.

At Levens Hall, Mrs Susan Bagot and Felicity Weaver.

At Longleat House, The Marquess of Bath, Viv Toop and Kate Harris.

At Muncaster Castle, Peter Frost-Pennington.

At Owlpen Manor, Sir Nicholas and Lady Mander, Jane Simmons and Rebecca Boeater.

At Powderham Castle, Lady Katherine Watney, Clare Crawshaw and Ingrid Oram.

At Prideaux Place, Mrs Elisabeth Prideaux-Brune and Carmen Hocking.

At Ripley Castle, Sir Thomas Ingilby Bt and Alison Crawford.

At Samlesbury Hall, Sarah Bradshaw.

At Sausmarez Manor, Peter de Sausmarez, Seigneur.

At Tissington Hall, Sir Richard FitzHerbert Bt and Maggie Nicholls.

At Traquair House, Ms Catherine Maxwell-Stuart.

At Whitmore Hall, Mrs Christine Cavenagh-Mainwaring.

At Woburn Abbey, The Duke of Bedford and Christopher Gravett.

Introduction

Although circumstances may prevent the ghosts in Britain's historic houses from being alive and well, judging by the many and varied contributions to the research for this book from members of the Historic Houses Association, they are certainly as active and busy as they have ever been.

'Ghosts' make their presence felt in all kinds of different ways. There are ubiquitous White Ladies and Grey Ladies, who take on so lifelike a form that many people who see them have no idea they have encountered a ghost until the lady in question passes through a hedge or a wall, or until someone throws a pillow or rides a bicycle right through her. Other houses have mischievous, ghostly children who delight in running up and down staircases, usually at night and invariably to the annoyance of the adults they wake up. Then there are those properties plagued by poltergeists responsible for creating upheaval and disturbance without any sign of who or what is responsible.

With houses dating back hundreds of years, the ghosts of occupants from many generations

back share their former homes with present-day owners and their families. However, not all ghosts originate in the distant past. In at least one instance a ghost of a former owner returned to the home he loved only a short time after his death, perhaps to check that all was well, though more likely in his case because the old habit of showing people around died hard. With such a rich catalogue of hauntings and supernatural goings-on, it's probably just as well that the majority of ghostly activities are benign; only in a small number of cases do they cause serious distress to the living.

On the other hand the ghosts of Britain's historic houses are a growing source of fascination to visitors and throughout the country many properties open to the general public are finding that ghost tours and all-night vigils are becoming increasingly popular. The ghosts, it would appear, are doing their bit to help maintain the time-honoured castles, mansions and manor houses that they inhabited during their own lifetime.

happy childhood memories of mastering saddle
and stirrup in a long-gone nursery mounted on

near the linen cupboard at the top of the back
stairs, although she could never quite hear what

was said. And while working in the sewing room, there were times when she was conscious of the sound of a child's humming, as if the child was happily entertaining herself while busy working at something. This humming could be heard quite strongly, even when Sandra had the radio on.

It is known that this part of the house, now the kitchen wing, was part of a workshop or factory for cloth-making up to the middle of the 17th century and it appears that the whole of the first floor, including the sewing room, was one large room where the cloth was stretched and processed. Perhaps the child humming was a young worker from this early factory or a young servant girl singing to herself as she went about her daily chores in this part of the house.

Sandra's young daughter used to play in Elizabeth Cartwright-Hignett's son William's playroom, which was in the same part of Iford Manor previously used for processing cloth. She would tell her mother that she felt someone watching her there and that on occasions she would hear the floorboards creak although no one was

around. Mrs Cartwright-Hignett has experienced this herself when on her own in the playroom.

William's nanny, during his first year, also used to tell that sometimes she would hear the sounds of a baby crying in an adjacent room even when she was with William, or when he was fast asleep.

The first floor seems to be the scene of several unexplained sightings. In the early 1970s Iford Manor was occupied by a doctor and his family: Harry, Pat and their two teenage children, Andrew and Kaira. One afternoon, while Pat was ironing in the kitchen, she looked up at the window on the first floor across the inner courtyard and caught a glimpse of a young girl with fair hair wearing a blue dress. The girl appeared to pass behind the window and Pat thought it was her daughter Kaira, who was also fair-haired. As she was aware that this particular ancient window was blocked up, having had a fireplace built behind it, Pat assumed that it was a reflection from the window at right angles to it on the stairs. She went on ironing. Some minutes later she realised that it could not possibly have been Kaira as she was still at school and she wouldn't be picking her up until later. Perhaps the ghostly figure wasn't a reflection from the window on the stairs after all but a glimpse of someone, or something, passing behind a long-blocked-up window.

Then there are accounts of youthful high spirits, of cheeky, impish, fun and games (frequently at the expense of adults) that current residents have grown accustomed to. Like many historic houses that welcome visitors through their doors **Kiplin Hall**, in North Yorkshire, caters for a wide spectrum of educational, hands-on activities for schools in a room that is also available for families to enjoy during the school holidays. However, the Education Room at Kiplin Hall has more to offer, as visitors and staff have discovered.

The room is located at the end of the Long Gallery and, in the 1890s, was used by the family governess; her young charges' nursery was in the adjacent room. In 2005, during one of Kiplin's regular family events, a young boy whispered to his mother that he could see a figure standing in the corner of the room. The boy was very calm

Education Room, Kiplin Hall

and obviously didn't wish to draw attention to himself, as he spoke very quietly to his mother. What the boy could not have been aware of was that the previous year a psychic investigator had seen a woman in the same room, dressed in dark grey and described as being 'very prim and proper' – as might be expected of a traditional Victorian governess.

Other unsettling, supernatural events suggest that she might not be alone in maintaining a presence in her former domain. Her young charges, or children of school-room age at any event, seem not to be above enjoying high jinks as the warden at Kiplin discovered when she also had a strange experience in this room.

She was tidying the room following an educational visit and had stacked all the children's chairs on the tables, before washing the floor. When she entered the room the following morning, all the chairs had been thrown from the tables and were scattered around the room, but no one had been in the Hall after she left the previous evening. This happened again one morning in March 2006, when the warden and a conservation volunteer (a retired head-teacher) were working in the Long Gallery. There was a tremendous sound of things crashing about in the Education Room and, when they went to investigate, once again the chairs, which had been neatly stacked on the tables, were lying all around on the floor.

When the psychic investigator made a second visit, she reported children moving the chairs, throwing them around and behaving mischievously. She again saw the figure of a woman who, one may presume, was the governess. She was wearing Victorian garments and stood to the right of the fireplace, or near the window seat beside the door opening into the Long Gallery. She may have appeared tall and very stern to the psychic investigator, but this did not prevent a group of children running amok, playing hide-and-seek, popping between the governess's room and the nursery, while the governess looked on. In addition, two small shadows appeared to be floating across the room. Could the children once kept in check by this formidable lady be getting their own back? It certainly seemed that way.

Susan Bagot who, with her husband Hal, has raised her own family at Levens Hall, in Cumbria, (well-populated with ghosts as is revealed later) voices an opinion shared by many parents who have brought up their offspring in houses where the past is always present. 'I think children have uncluttered minds,' she comments, 'and see things that adults don't see.' That would certainly account for the 'governess' seen by the little boy at Kiplin – and for similar instances of children being

Long Gallery, Kiplin Hall

aware of the presence of others who remain invisible to adults in the room.

But children do not have a monopoly in this respect. One of the ghosts at **Prideaux Place**, at Padstow in Cornwall, is described by Elisabeth Prideaux-Brune as 'a little pantry boy, who rushes off into the small pantry off the kitchen, to which there is no other exit.' The first time she saw his crouched figure she was convinced it was her youngest son, William, who would have been about ten at the time. 'I remember distinctly that he was wearing a kind of beige jerkin,' she continues. 'Will was always playing practical jokes, so I assumed it was him hiding in the pantry. So I

15

Great Chamber, Prideaux Place

16

said, "Come on, Will, I know you're in there."' But, of course, her son wasn't to be seen, nor was anyone else; the pantry was empty.

She describes the pantry boy as completely friendly, 'You don't feel threatened by him at all,' and this is an impression left by many child ghosts. Asked whether her husband or sons had seen the same figure, Mrs Prideaux-Brune gives another prescient reply:'I've always heard – and I don't know how true it is – that quite often people who grow up in a house don't see the ghosts. It's people who marry in or inherit the house as adults.'

Karin, Lady Mander, is another mother who has had to contend with the mischievous offspring of past generations as well as her own family. When she and her husband, Sir Nicholas, married in the mid-1970s they set up home at **Owlpen Manor**, near Uley in the Cotswolds. At least 900 years old, standing in its own romantic, wood-flanked valley, Owlpen Manor is regarded as one of the most haunted houses in Gloucestershire, with traditions that associate it with at least four resident ghosts.

One of them, described by Lady Mander as 'the mischievous child', appears to be a little girl who delights in running up and down the back stairs, often waking guests who were previously enjoying an unbroken sleep. Owlpen is unusual too in possessing a photograph that seems to support her spectral presence in the house. Taken from the garden, at a time when the house was known to be empty, it shows a young child's face peering from an oriel window upstairs.

Extraordinary photograph of a ghostly child's face peering through the window at Owlpen Manor

To Lady Mander, there is no mystery. 'They exist … or something exists,' she maintains. And she should know. Friends and guests have become so alarmed at the prospect of staying in certain parts of the house, that they opt to sleep in probably the most cramped bedroom, rather than enjoy the comfort and space of the medieval solar and other rooms in which they feel distinctly uncomfortable. 'I'm running out of bedrooms,' Lady Mander explains. (It looks as if an exorcism is called for, but the reasons for that must wait until later in this book.)

Children (living ones this time) feature as significant witnesses to Owlpen's most prestigious ghost: Queen Margaret of Anjou. During the Wars of the Roses, the 'ardent queen' and consort of Henry VI, reputedly stayed at Owlpen on her way to the fateful Battle of Tewkesbury, which was fought on 2 May 1471. The Daunt family, resident at Owlpen at the time, were supporters of the House of Lancaster. Queen Margaret's son, the Prince of Wales, had written to them asking for help in mustering troops for his father's cause, so it seems likely that Queen Margaret could

Queen Margaret's Room, Owlpen Manor

have come to Owlpen, where the Great Chamber (above the Great Hall) is known as Queen Margaret's Room.

Though different in appearance to the way she would have known it, the room is said to be haunted by her ghost, if for no other reason than that she probably spent the last happy night of her life there. The Lancastrian forces were routed at the battle which followed, both her husband and son were cruelly murdered in the aftermath and Queen Margaret eked out the rest of her sad life exiled in France, widowed and, by the standards of a medieval queen, penniless.

At Owlpen she retains her regal splendour, glimpsed as the phantom of a grey lady, dressed in a fur-trimmed gown, with a steeple hat and wimple – and this is where the children enter her story, as unwitting witnesses. During the Second World War child evacuees from Birmingham were billeted in the area around Owlpen and a few fortunate ones found themselves living in the medieval manor house itself, which was then the home of Barbara Bray. The American architectural historian, Francis Comstock, writing some time later, takes up the story:

One night, in making her customary round, she looked in to see that the four children were sleeping; she found them all awake and excited; they told her of their visitor, 'a lovely lady with long sleeves and dress all trimmed with fur, and with a funny peaked hat that had a long veil hanging down behind' – a description of such a costume as Queen Margaret might have worn, and of which the children must have been completely ignorant.

Moving from the Middle Ages to the 18th century, and from the Cotswolds to the Channel Islands, a similar story is told of a night-time visitor, only visible to children, who resides at **Sausmarez Manor** on Guernsey. Peter de Sausmarez, present-day Seigneur and custodian of the house, tells of his experiences with the 'nanny of the twenty-eight children'. They lived in the house during the time of his ancestor Thomas John de Sausmarez, occupying the nursery quarters on the top-most floor in the early 19th century. Peter first made the

Nanny of the 28 children, Sausmarez Manor

acquaintance of the nanny when he found the portrait of a 'little old lady' shortly after moving in and hung it on a wall in the small hall in the 18th-century part of the house. At that time his elderly cousin and his wife (from whom he ultimately inherited Sausmarez Manor) occupied the lower part of the house and it was they who identified the portrait as that of the 'nanny of the twenty-eight children', with whom they were delighted to be reunited, her portrait having been mislaid.

Some time later, when Peter's wife had to be away in England for a few days and he was looking after their young sons William and Rollo aged five and four, he accepted a last-minute invitation to a drinks party and installed the teenage daughter of a friend to act as a temporary babysitter. It didn't take his little boys long to realise that they could run this poor girl ragged and when their father returned he found the house in uproar and the erstwhile babysitter hot, bothered and completely at her wits' end. After reading the two little horrors the riot act, Peter drove the poor girl home. But coming back up the drive to the house he was horrified to see it blazing with light from top to bottom: the boys were still at it.

However, a thorough and rather testy search of the house revealed no sign of them. They weren't hiding in any of their usual haunts. In fact the house was quiet. After looking under beds and behind curtains, switching off the lights as he went, Peter thought he should check their bedroom, having left it to last because it seemed highly unlikely that they would be there after running riot in the house … or so it seemed.

To his complete surprise he found them both in bed just dropping off to sleep.

Why were all the lights on, their father wanted to know?

'Daddy, we were so frightened,' they told him. 'We didn't know where you were. We were looking for you everywhere.'

Then why were they so calm and relaxed when their father found them, he asked?

'Oh, it was all right,' they explained. 'The little old lady came along, read us a story and tucked us into bed.'

Imagining that his cousin had been kind enough to restore order, Peter popped through the interconnecting door to their part of the house the next morning to thank her and apologise for the havoc the children must have been causing while he had been out the previous evening.

But his cousin said she hadn't heard a thing. Perhaps her daughter had gone up to sort out the little boys?

Since she was 'a damsel of some 25 summers' Peter went through to the wing where she lived, to ask with some trepidation whether she might possibly have put his boys to bed.

'Oh, no. It wasn't me,' she said, adding, 'Did they by any chance say if it was a little old lady?'

With considerable embarrassment, Peter had to confirm that they had. But his cousin's daughter was totally unfazed by the association and told him, 'That's all right, then. That's the nanny of the twenty-eight children. It used to happen to us quite often when we were children.'

'I didn't believe a word she was saying,' Peter continues. 'So I hastily rang up her sister, who was at work, and asked "What's all this about the nanny?"'

'Has she reappeared?' was the enthusiastic question at the other end of the line. 'Because she often used to look after us when we were children.'

As far as Peter was concerned, that provided confirmation enough – and he gleefully anticipated a free babysitter into the bargain.

However, the nanny went back into spiritual retirement until about ten years later, when Peter was now on his own in his part of the house. Almost without exception, friends who came to stay wanted to know whether the house was haunted.

When he asked why they were interested, every one replied that they had met an old woman on their way to and from the bathroom during the night, who had told them to take care of Peter.

Children, it would seem, are not her sole concern at Sausmarez Manor.

Medieval consorts and 18th-century nannies are not the only spectral guardians of small children in Britain's historic houses. From **Ripley Castle**, in Yorkshire, Sir Thomas Ingilby describes events during the time that he and his wife, Emma, have been living in the Castle, which has been the Ingilby family home for almost 700 years. He relates:

In recent years our guides have twice seen a lady in 19th-century costume walk across the landing at the top of the main staircase, before passing through a locked door. The two sightings happened in broad daylight within a fortnight of each other, but she hasn't been seen for four or five years since.

When my wife was breastfeeding our children, she frequently used to fall asleep in the dressing room, on the bed next to the cot. If the baby started stirring, my wife could feel someone – or something – tugging anxiously at her sleeve, as if to say 'Wake up – your baby needs you'.

Lady Alicia Ingilby lost her son and daughter to meningitis in the 1870s: we think that she must

Knight's Chamber, Ripley Castle

still be caring for the children of the house in spirit, and that it was her image that the guides saw passing across the landing. She is certainly a friendly presence.

Friendly too is the 'nanny ghost' who appears from time to time at **Chillingham Castle** in Northumberland. The circumstances surrounding her appearance always involve a family staying in rooms high in the Look-out Tower. In the small hours of the morning, the parents will be woken to the sounds of their children romping and rampaging in their bed. The parents, not best pleased at having their sleep rudely interrupted, storm in to find out what is going on, to be told that their children were woken by two other children sneaking into the room and tickling their toes. Then they started playing games.

Seeing their children excited and thoroughly awake, the parents invariably take the children down to the kitchen for a glass of milk and a talking-to and then to the bathroom. Whatever happens, the family leave the children's bedroom.

When they return, with the kids calm again and more inclined to go to sleep, they find that the previously rumpled sheets and bedding are beautifully smooth and inviting.

The spectral nanny has also been disturbed, it would seem. And, having packed her two charges back to their beds, has made amends with her young guests and tidied their beds before they return. Mischievous some of these child spirits may be, but they never appear to be malevolent. These playful spectres are still at it today!

Children, more specifically the suffering of children – even those long dead – can be unbearably sad and very frightening when it wakes you suddenly during the night.

In the Middle Ages wrongdoers of any age were hanged from ancient yew trees in the Chillingham Castle approaches, their disintegrating bodies left to the elements and scavenging wildlife. It is said that other unfortunate victims were hanged around the outer walls of the Castle to scare away would-be assailants, and Chillingham's gruesome relics of punishment and retribution show that children as well as adults suffered the cruel 'justice' meted out in the Castle during centuries of conflict along the Scottish border.

The Castle chapel, situated in the base of one of the two original medieval square towers around which the Castle has grown, is the domain of the ghost of a girl known as Eleanor. She was no doubt one of innumerable victims of the raids and kidnappings, which took place both sides of the border in the Middle Ages. Brought as a captive to Chillingham, she may have been incarcerated in the Castle's terrible dungeon. Whatever her fate, Eleanor appears to have been released, but having nowhere to go, she took shelter in what is now the chapel where she probably died of cold and hunger, frightened and alone.

As a result, her tormented soul makes regular appearances during tours of the Castle. Women in particular have been aware of someone tugging at the sleeves of their clothing. A curtain covering a door has been seen moving for no apparent reason. Prayer books and hymn books have been moved from their shelves; others have slowly

Chillingham Castle

slipped from tables and pews to fall to the floor. Some female visitors wearing their hair in ponytails have even felt these being lifted by an unseen presence. Centuries on from her own time, young Eleanor remains deeply curious about those who have come after her to this ancient chapel.

Perhaps Chillingham's most famous apparition makes his presence felt in the upper floors of the Castle, where what has always been known as the Pink Room, is said to be haunted by The Radiant (or Blue) Boy. He used to appear as a bright halo of light close to a passage cut through the ten- feet thick wall into the adjoining tower. Those who encountered him in the Pink Room were woken by the pitiful wailing of a child close to the old four-poster bed where they slept. This was followed by the chilling sight of a boy, dressed in blue and surrounded by light, gently approaching. A number of witnesses reported that the boy was dressed in clothes similar to those worn during the Restoration period in the second half of the 17th century, when King Charles II was on the throne.

During the 1920s, builders working in the Pink Room discovered the bones of what turned out to be a young boy, together with some fragments of blue fabric. His remains were removed and buried in consecrated ground, since when the whole figure has not been seen again. However, to this day guests staying in the Pink Room have reported occasional blue flashes at night, when they have been in bed. The immediate suspicions, that these are the result of faulty electrical wiring, are readily dismissed by the fact that there are no electrical fittings of any kind in the wall where the flashes are always seen. Although the mortal remains of the Radiant Boy were laid to rest nearly ninety years ago, his spiritual attachment to the Pink Room at Chillingham Castle remains undimmed, or is some small bone fragment left in the masonry?

Muncaster Castle, near Ravenglass in Cumbria, home to the Pennington family for 800 years, is another ancient fortification, which, like Chillingham, once guarded the wild borderland between England and Scotland. Like Chillingham too, Muncaster has one particular bedroom where guests may well experience something out of the ordinary. As Peter Frost-Pennington, one of those now living in the Castle, explains, the family had to give up using the Tapestry Room as guest accommodation because so many people spent disturbed and uncomfortable nights in there; many being kept awake for long hours of the night by the sounds of a baby or a child crying.

Although the Tapestry Room is no longer used to house family guests, it has proved to be extremely popular with small parties of people who spend the night there on vigils. Groups of friends, occasionally from overseas, wanting to experience a different kind of night out, serious students of the paranormal and scientific colleagues of Dr Jason Braithwaite of Birmingham University, who has undertaken a closely observed study of the phenomena at Muncaster Castle – dozens of people over several years have recorded a surprisingly similar set of sights and sounds during their time in the Tapestry Room. Rattling doors, handles turning when no one is there, a power failure in cameras, camcorders, laptops and other electronic equipment, feelings of chest pains or chest constriction, and crying or wailing

occur in many accounts recorded in Muncaster's 'Ghost-sitters Book'. Entries from June 2003 sum up what many visitors have felt:

I had a weird experience in the four-poster bed. I felt that my body was touched and for a split second I was unable to make a noise! And I couldn't control a flow of tears for about 45 minutes afterwards … A very eerie, heart-pounding night! We heard what sounded very much like a baby cry then suddenly stop! That was enough for us to leave the Tapestry Room and stay in the dressing room all night.

The Tapestry Room at Muncaster may have this effect on most adults, but at least one child had a

The Tapestry Room, Muncaster Castle

very different response to her experiences there. She was the four-year-old daughter of one of the cleaners, who accompanied her mother occasionally when her child-minder was unable to look after her. This child's story is particularly interesting.

The little girl was with her mother one day while she was in the Tapestry Room, when a picture was knocked over. Her mother naturally ticked off her daughter, telling her to be more careful. But her daughter said she hadn't touched the picture; it was the little girl she was playing with who had accidentally knocked it over. As far as her mother was concerned, of course, there wasn't another child in the room and she put down the episode with the picture to a bit of quick thinking on her daughter's part and the timely creation of an imaginary friend to take the blame.

The imaginary friend started to become very real. Even at home, the little girl asked for a place to be laid for her at the table and for a portion of food to be offered to her as well. Then a television company investigating ghosts at Muncaster asked

whether the cleaner's daughter might be willing to appear on camera to tell her story and describe the little girl she played with. Her mother asked her, but her daughter declined: though not out of shyness. The reason she gave was that she didn't want to do anything 'to scare Susan away'.

'So I asked her, "Who's Susan?"' says Peter Frost-Pennington.

'Susan is the name of the girl she plays with in that bedroom,' the little girl's mother explained.

Was the invisible child's name a coincidence? Who can say? It does seem unlikely, though, that a four-year-old would have been aware of a possible connection between a real Susan and Muncaster Castle.

'We think the child,' Peter Frost-Pennington explains, 'is the only child of the Fourth Lord Muncaster, who died in 1871 at the age of 11, of what was described as screaming fits. She was called Margaret Susan Elizabeth Pennington. We always refer to her as Margaret and to me it was quite bizarre that a child as young as four could come up with the name of the girl – and not the common name you would expect. And she loved being in that room – loved playing there.'

Eyam Hall in the Derbyshire Peak District is another historic house with a haunted Tapestry Room. The home of the Wright family for over 300 years, it was also the home of the 'girl in the red dress' during her short time on earth. As Nicola Wright, whose family live in Eyam Hall today, relates, this was Georgina, the elder sister of John Wright and the granddaughter of John and Elizabeth Wright, who built Eyam Hall shortly after the Great Plague of 1665–6, which claimed the lives of eight out of ten villagers in a matter of months.

Their mother died giving birth to John and when John and Georgina were three and eight respectively, their father also died. It was left to their guardian Charles Potts to bring them up. Georgina was a spirited and intelligent child and had been highly regarded by her parents; however she suffered from a mild form of epilepsy when she would 'switch off' from what was happening around her for several seconds. Unfortunately for

Eyam Hall

her, Charles was not fond of girls and in particular of highly intelligent little girls.

Charles had a reputation for taking risks with his own business and proceeded to run the Eyam Hall Estate on the same basis. Before long he started to sell the contents of the house to cover his losses. Georgina, seeing her and her brother's inheritance being squandered, started to ask Charles embarrassing questions about his dealings. Charles retaliated by spreading a rumour that Georgina was possessed by demons and her strange absences were in fact when she was communicating with the devil himself. The servants, being superstitious country folk, started to regard Georgina as a frightening presence and therefore did not intervene when Charles locked her up for long periods in

29

the Tapestry Room. This was a particularly cruel punishment as Georgina was convinced it was haunted by the people in the tapestries; in particular she was absolutely terrified by the dripping head of Holofernes depicted in one of the pictures. Of course the fact that she thought she could see ghosts lent even more weight to Charles's theory that she was consorting with the devil.

One dark evening Georgina was again shut in the Tapestry Room for some minor misdemeanour. She had screamed for hours and battered at the door with her little fists until they were bruised and bleeding, but the servants dared do nothing to help her and her guardian ignored the noise. Finally there was silence then a terrible scream followed by a dull thud on the terrace below the Tapestry Room window. The servants rushed outside where a terrible sight met their eyes. The little girl lay dead on the ground; her eyes were open and terrified and she was covered in blood from injuries caused by trying to escape the room that had become her prison.

Her death led to the removal of Charles, as many questions were asked and the servants told of his cruelties to Georgina. Bars were put up at all the opening windows on the first floor but it was too late to save the little girl who had dared to ask too many questions of her guardian.

Late at night, guests who stay in the Tapestry Room report that the window opens on its own and a shadowy figure in a red dress is seen standing at the window. Suddenly the figure disappears and an eerie scream pierces the night.

Twenty-five miles to the south of Eyam, **Tissington Hall,** near Ashbourne, was the scene of a childhood tragedy for the FitzHerbert family, who have been living at Tissington for over 500 years. The victim of this sad event was Mina FitzHerbert who died in 1862 and it is she who is principally responsible for the hauntings in the house.

Sir Richard FitzHerbert, the ninth consecutive baronet to live in the Hall, knows more than anyone about its supernatural occupants. He is 'one of two people to have slept the night on my own in this 48-chimney, 61-room, seven-staircase and seven-bathroom house, that usually houses my family, three dogs, two cats, two guinea pigs, mice, rats and a colony of bats'.

Tissington Hall

Staircase at Tissington Hall

'The main story,' he continues, 'is about one of my ancestors who caught fire from a burning candle in the 1860s and subsequently died of the injuries she sustained.' This was Mina FitzHerbert, whose nightdress was set alight by a candle when she opened her bedroom windows one night in the summer of 1862. Writing to his mother on 20 August 1862, Sir William FitzHerbert described what happened:

My Dear Mother

Last night a terrible accident happened to Mina … It was from being on fire by opening a window of her bedroom. She sat down and tried to get up the rug … The rug unhappily was tacked down so was useless. She then rolled herself onto the bed but alas only set the bed on fire. Becca heard her and ran onto the stairs and shrieked. I found Annie just dragging Mina into the gallery all in flame. Annie's large dress rolled round her and with some water the fire was put out.

She is severely burnt but I hope some of the burns are not deep, as very large blisters have come up. Mr Goodwin says she has no more fever than must be. We had some work to get the fire down in the room.

Poor Mina says how often I have warned them about fire. I hope that if no unfavourable symptoms come out that in a day or two the danger will be passed.

Six days later he reported:

Last night the opiate and chloroform seemed to take great effect and she slept from about 10.30 till 2. Mina has said to Becca she thinks she is better today and freer from pain. She has had tea and some beef tea also, and iced water. Mrs Hardy who is always back and forward is very well.

The story goes on until a letter of 4 September, which records Mina's death.

'Subsequently it is her "ghost" that has been reported to me,' explains Sir Richard, 'and has been seen on various occasions by members of the family over the years.' When 21st-century paranormal investigators conducted research in the course of a 'ghost evening', they made reference to Mina and found their video camera batteries 'going flat' when they entered the area where she had died.

Sad as her fate was, Sir Richard feels quite at ease to be sharing his home with one of its former occupants. 'I believe Mina is a benevolent "ghost",' he says, 'and I personally am very fond of her.'

Cloistered Existence

Turn back the clock 500 years and, alongside the crown, the nobility and an emerging class of wealthy landowners, the church owned and farmed large estates. By the time Henry VIII ascended the throne resentment was building against this monastic hierarchy.

Under pressure from such critics and as his own argument with the church grew over his wish to divorce Katherine of Aragon, Henry acquiesced and in 1536 what became known as the Dissolution of the Monasteries began. The great religious houses in England were systematically closed down and their estates taken over by the king, who by now had declared himself Supreme Head of the Church in England. Hundreds of years of tradition and ordered practice were swept away, and those in holy orders who had enjoyed the security of their cloistered, monastic existence found themselves pensioned off and flung into a secular world of which they had little experience and in which they no longer had a part to play.

Most went quietly, if grudgingly, but there were those who maintained to the end their resistance to the king's wholesale hijacking of the church and many such protesters paid a heavy price. Among them was Robert Hobbes, the last abbot of **Woburn Abbey** in Bedfordshire. He had been bold enough to speak out publicly against Henry's activities, in particular his divorce of his first wife, Katherine of Aragon, in order to free himself to marry his second, Anne Boleyn.

Henry did not bear such opposition lightly. While eleven of the monks residing at Woburn Abbey were sent on their way, the king's commissioners summarily tried the abbot and two other senior

clergy, finding them guilty of treason. They then reputedly hanged them from the boughs of a tree at the Abbey gate. Legend holds that this tree is the great oak still growing in the park in direct sight of the present-day house; it is now known as the Abbot's Oak.

No one will ever know whether the last abbot of Woburn laid a curse on the abbey and those who would own it after him, but sightings of the ghostly figure of a monk have been widely reported in different parts of the house to the present day.

The 15th, and current, Duke of Bedford recalls 'a weird event' that has lodged in his mind. He explains how his father had a huge stroke in 1988 and that some time afterwards a very well-known divining lady came to lunch. When she walked into the room, which had been his father's office and is now a sitting room, she exclaimed that there was the most dreadful ley line going through the room.

Tracing the line from his chair, where he was sitting when he had his stroke, she followed it all the way back up to the Abbot's Oak in the park, where she drove a copper tube into the ground to get rid of it.

The Duke of Bedford is also well acquainted with unexplained sightings at Woburn. 'In the 1980s,' he

Woburn Abbey

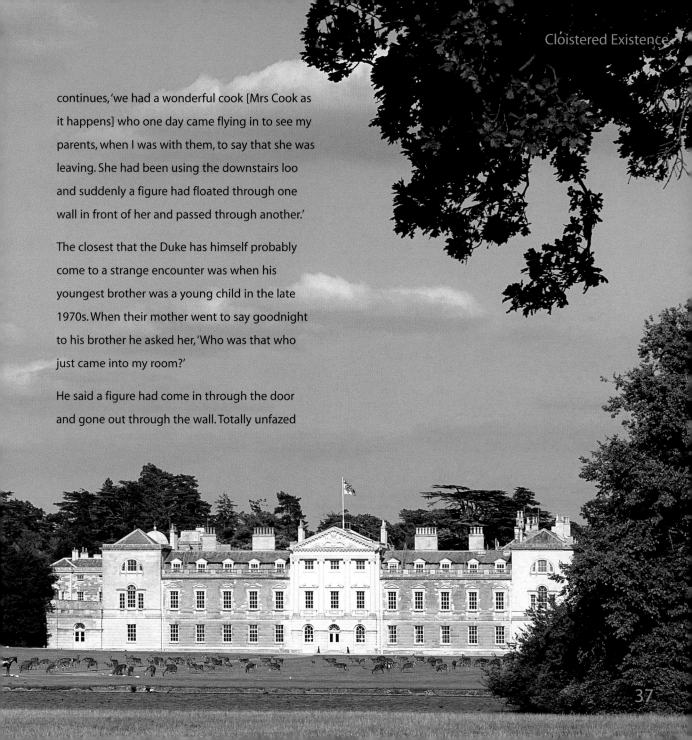

continues, 'we had a wonderful cook [Mrs Cook as it happens] who one day came flying in to see my parents, when I was with them, to say that she was leaving. She had been using the downstairs loo and suddenly a figure had floated through one wall in front of her and passed through another.'

The closest that the Duke has himself probably come to a strange encounter was when his youngest brother was a young child in the late 1970s. When their mother went to say goodnight to his brother he asked her, 'Who was that who just came into my room?'

He said a figure had come in through the door and gone out through the wall. Totally unfazed by it, he said the figure was wearing a long brown coat all the way to the floor and had a brown hat pulled over its head. If you think what a monk would wear, you couldn't get a closer description.

Before the Dissolution, **Beaulieu** in Hampshire, like Woburn, had been an abbey with an abbot and a community of monks belonging to the Cistercian order, which had broken away from the Benedictines at the end of the 11th century to observe the rule of St Benedict more strictly. The Cistercians founded their abbey at Beaulieu in 1204 and many of the monastic features that evolved there over the next 300 years – including the cloister, the Domus (where the lay monks lived), the refectory (now the parish church, where the choir monks ate) and the Great Gatehouse (where guests were received and which is now the nucleus of the present-day Palace House) – remain, as, it appears, do a number of the abbey's original occupants.

Although the last official abbot left Beaulieu in the spring of 1538 with an annual pension of 66 pounds, 13 shillings and four pence (£66.66) there

was a self-styled 'Abbot of Beaulieu' officiating as a priest 400 years later. This was the eccentric Robert Frazer Powles, the last 'independent' vicar of Beaulieu, before the church came under diocesan control in 1939.

The Revd Powles was Vicar of Beaulieu from 1886 and, free from the control of any bishop, he took full advantage of the scope this gave him. Dressing himself in an abbot's robes and mitre was only part of the pleasure he took in his post. Associating with the ghost monks of Beaulieu became a normal part of the Revd Powles's life as well. 'People got to asking him how they were,' Lord Montagu, whose home Beaulieu is, told one investigator in the early 1960s, 'and he would reply: "Oh, Brother Norman was sick today" or something like that. He even held special services just for them, usually on Christmas Eve.' When a parishioner commented to the vicar during the First World War that the service he had just taken was rather thinly attended, he replied, 'It's bigger than you can see'. To his eyes at least the pews were well filled with his ghostly predecessors in holy orders.

Dining Room, Beaulieu

Parish Church, Beaulieu

During the Second World War, Beaulieu served as a top-secret training centre for Allied agents about to be sent to work under cover in occupied Europe. Security was at a premium and the estate was closely guarded. Even so, more than one officer stationed there reported seeing a brown-clad monk, wandering freely inside the security cordon.

'The ghosts here have never been evil,' Lord Montagu told his interviewer. 'In fact, they've never been anything but extremely friendly, and they have been seen and heard by countless people.'

Their presence is also signalled by a particular smell: catching a whiff of the strong aroma of incense is not uncommon at Beaulieu.

For many years Miss Aimée Cheshire lived in a flat in the former Domus, where she frequently heard the sound of monks at their devotions. Not long after her death, a Mrs Samuels, the elderly nurse companion of another former member of staff, was standing outside her flat overlooking the ruined cloisters when she saw a monk standing in the fifth archway along. She noticed that he was

holding a scroll and she was able to watch him for several minutes before he disappeared.

Another resident of the estate forty years ago was Colonel Robert Gore-Browne, who described seeing a ghost himself. 'I was taking the dog out for a walk round about dusk, following the lane that goes past this house,' he began. 'Some way ahead and walking towards me I saw a figure in brown, with a skirt that reached down to the ground.

'I thought it was a woman, actually. I only had to go down a small dip and up again before we passed each other. But when I got to the brow of the little hill there wasn't anybody there. I looked either side of the path and I'm pretty sure she wasn't there, either.'

Michael Sedgwick, a leading automotive historian in his day, worked with Lord Montagu in the early days of what was then called the Montagu Motor Museum. As its Research Director he was a man more inclined to engineering and science than the supernatural. Even so, his account of what he heard at Beaulieu echoes the experiences of many others.

41

'The first time I heard it was just before Christmas 1959. I had a lot of work to do and had been up typing and chain-smoking until the early hours. I decided to open the windows and air the room a bit before I went to bed.

'When I opened the window I heard it quite distinctly: it was definitely chanting, and very beautiful chanting. It came in uneven waves, as if from a faulty wireless – sometimes quite loud and then fading away. It was just as if a Catholic Mass was being played on the radio in the next flat, but I thought that it was curious that someone should have the radio on at that time of night. Anyway, it was so beautiful that I tried to find it on my own wireless. I tell you, I went through every blessed programme there was – French, Italian, everything – and I couldn't find it. Later I was told it was just a common or garden supernatural phenomenon. And as a matter of fact it had occurred on the night that someone in the village had died.

'The second time I heard it I was also up late working, and also on the eve of a burial. I didn't bother to try and pick it up on the wireless that time.'

Michael Sedgwick was not the only person to hear chanting at Beaulieu that winter night. The catering manageress at the time, Mrs Bertha Day, was aware of it when she came home late. 'Suddenly I heard this singing, just like a service being held in the church. I knew that Mrs Mears, a local lady, had died. The following day I asked the vicar if he had held any kind of requiem service for her – just to make sure. He said he hadn't. It was lovely singing, I'll always remember it – it gave you a wonderful feeling of peace.'

About a year later the sounds of what did appear to be a burial were heard by Michael Sedgwick and his mother. 'Our sitting room window overlooked a piece of ground which is believed to be the monks' burial ground,' he said. 'It's on the north-east side of the church where, traditionally, the monks always put their dead.

'We were sitting there one night when, through the window, came the sounds of feet walking slowly and heavily as if men were carrying a heavy

burden. You could hear every bit of their progress, even the different sound their footsteps made when they crossed the bridge over the stream. When we looked out we couldn't see a thing, but the sounds came very close until there were thumps and thuds as if someone was digging in the garden.

'Since, I believe, monks usually carried out their funerals at night, it seems likely we were hearing the re-enactment of a burial.'

Lord Montagu's half-sister, the Hon Mrs Varley, grew up in the Palace House at Beaulieu, which she found very frightening at times. Even as a young woman, sitting at an open window on a hot summer night, she was still susceptible to Beaulieu's haunting mysteries.

'I was so deep in my thoughts that it had been going on for quite a while before I became conscious of it. What made me first aware of it was the frissons of cold that started running up and down my back. It was the sound of many voices in repetitive singing, which faded and strengthened like the sound of a primitive wireless. At first I thought it was a wireless in the servants' hall.

'But the sound wasn't coming from there. I couldn't tell you where it *was* coming from. Then the dog began to howl and I got really frightened. I jumped into bed and pulled the sheets right over me. The Peke hid under the eiderdown.

'The next morning I told everybody what I had heard and they tried to laugh me out of it and said I'd probably heard gypsies singing. But an archaeologist friend who was staying with us said that as far as he knew there weren't any gypsies in the neighbourhood, and asked me to sing the tune to him. It was pretty well carved into my memory, so I sang it. He told me it was a well-known Gregorian chant.'

The experience of what she heard so preyed on Mrs Varley's mind that she went to see Miss Cheshire, whom she described as being 'very psychic'. Unsure how to broach the subject, Mrs Varley began picking out the melody of the chant on Miss Cheshire's piano, while she prepared tea. 'So you heard it too,' Aimée Cheshire said to her visitor .'It was so loud last night, that I thought someone else besides myself would hear it.'

Although Elisabeth Cartwight-Hignett may not have been raised as a child at **Iford Manor**, having lived there for over 40 years she is well acquainted with its past and the impact this still has on Iford today.

When she made her first visits there in the spring of 1964, it was still the home of Sir Michael and Lady Peto, and Mrs Cartwright-Hignett was captivated by the house and gardens. Taking a walk by herself after lunch one day, she became aware of a strong smell of incense. 'When I got back to the house,' she continues, 'I asked Sir Michael what plant could be producing the scent. He looked a little embarrassed and said, rather hastily, that it would be the "curry bush" (*Sarcocca ruscifolia*) growing, as it still does, by the front gates. I thought no more about it until I sniffed the appropriate bush on our way out and realised that it was a different smell, quite apart from it being in the wrong part of the garden.

'Since then, this smell of incense has been noticed on many occasions and by a variety of different people. It has turned up all the over the place – from the great terrace to the far end of the kitchen garden, by the front door, by the cloister, on the patio garden terraces, inside as well as outside the house but more often than not in the garden. Another curious feature is that the smell remains steady in a wind and does not come and go like smoke from a bonfire.

'…The smell is quite unmistakably that of good quality incense, recognisable from High Mass at any Roman Catholic church, and is not to be confused with wood smoke, "curry bushes" or the outfall from the gas flue. It does not seem to be particular about the season and people seem most likely to experience it when in an open and thoughtful frame of mind. Whatever the nature or cause of this phenomenon, it is a happy one and I hope it remains with us.'

Her analysis chimes with that of many who have encountered vestiges of former occupants and occupations in historic houses. She writes:

Iford Manor cloisters

If the history of a place has any connection with the appearance of unexplained happenings, and there is considerable evidence that this is so, then it may be plausible to suppose that the smell of incense at Iford is related to some local connection with Roman Catholicism. During the 1300s, Iford, or at least part of it, was owned by the Carthusian monastery at Hinton Charterhouse, less than a mile away ...
It is probable that the lay brethren from Friary, a hamlet in Friary Wood across the river, may have managed Iford Mill for the monastery since they ran all the other support systems for them and they were operating the small mill at Friary itself. Local tradition has it that the bridge at Iford was originally built over the ford by the monks, and that they also provided the services for the chapel at Farleigh Castle at the other end of the valley.

Collinson, in his History of Somerset *of the late 18th century, states that there was a chapel at Iford until a few years before his visit here and that there was a cloister as well.*

... In the late 1980s, our housekeeper complained regularly that she was sure that the boot room near the side door was haunted. When she was in the kitchen she was aware on many occasions of the sound of the boot room door being opened when she knew no one was there. She had trouble, too, with the cellar door: if she shut it, unlocked, when she went off in the evening, she would find it open again in the morning. This phenomenon did not seem to occur in the daytime. She also saw a strange, unidentified figure on the drive one morning. She called someone to look, but the figure had gone.

Fleeting and often unseen as the cause of these phenomena may have been, there have been definite sightings of spectral presences at Iford. When Mrs Cartwright-Hignett first came to Iford, she asked the Petos if there were any unexplained phenomena, ghosts or suchlike that they had heard about or experienced themselves. They said that the only one they were aware of was the apparition of a monk which had been seen intermittently over a period of a year in different parts of the valley. This was related in particular to Friary Wood. Also a monk had been seen in Norton St Philip, which purports to have a tunnel leading from the George Inn – which was built by the monks as a wool market – to

Chavenage House

their abbey at Hinton Charterhouse. In 1991, the *Bath Chronicle* reported the apparition of a monk at a recently re-opened tunnel half a mile from Iford at Peradin's factory, which had originally been Freshford cloth mill.

One weekend in the 1970s, when he and his wife were staying at Iford, one of Mrs Cartwright-Hignett's guests saw the figure of a monk at the top of the stairs in Iford Mill. The monk wore a white habit and was described as having the eyes of a visionary with a face of great joy. Her friend only told her of this encounter some ten years after it had occurred as he said he had been embarrassed to mention it. He had felt that the apparition was entirely benevolent and that it was associated with the smell of incense, which occurred at the same time.

Follow the limestone escarpment of south-west England northwards from Iford and you reach **Chavenage House**, near Tetbury in Gloucestershire, which also has medieval monastic origins. Augustinian monks from Tours in France settled in the area following the

Norman Conquest and by the end of the 11th century a community of English monks had been established there. Parts of the present-day house, which was radically rebuilt in the 16th century, still date from this early medieval period. When these monastic holdings were acquired by the crown following Henry VIII's Dissolution of the Monasteries, the monks were dispersed. But after four centuries of residency their legacy was less easily swept away – if sightings over the years are to be believed at least one monk refuses to leave Chavenage altogether.

David Lowsley-Williams, who delights in sharing the stories of his family's home with visitors, is a lucid and engaging raconteur of unexplained sightings at Chavenage that people have passed on to him over the years.

'In 1945, just before the diocese took on a certain amount of responsibility for the chapel,' he will tell you, 'we had to find our own padre to take services. For a long time it was fairly easy, because there were so many RAF stations around and their chaplains were more than willing to come and do it. We had one of these young RAF padres taking a service and I heard him ask my uncle at dinner on the Saturday night (he'd come for the weekend) whether there was a monastery close by.

'And my uncle said, "No – not now."

'Then this young padre said, "Well, that's very strange. Just before dinner I went into the chapel to say some prayers and all the time I was in one of the pews, there was a monk knelt at the altar rail. I wanted to go up and tap him on the shoulder and ask him where he'd come from. But he seemed to be so engrossed in his prayers that I didn't like to disturb him. So, I tiptoed out of the door and left him to his praying."

'A few years ago we had a party of spiritualists, who asked if they could go round the house on their own. I caught up with them after about an hour and asked them if they had been having an interesting time.

'They said, "Oh, yes – especially in the chapel. We went into the chapel and we contacted a monk. He told us his name was Brother Charles, not to worry about his first name because it was rather difficult to pronounce, but just to call him Brother Charles and to tell people that he was very happy and content here at Chavenage."'

The chapel is not the only place at Chavenage where a monk has been seen. In an interview he gave in October 2006, David Lowsley-Williams spoke of another sighting made by a visitor to the house. Outside on the path, a very down-to-earth Australian was taking his dog for a walk when he passed a monk going up towards the chapel. The monk gave a sort of bow to him before carrying on. The visiting Australian had thought that anything to do with ghosts was a load of codswallop – but after that he wasn't so sure.

There also appears to be a ghostly monk on the **Knowsley Hall** estate, Lord Derby's family home near Liverpool. This gains some credence from the local tradition that a monastery once stood on nearby Riding Hill, although there is nothing to be seen of it now except for some stonework leading into a blocked-up passage. This passage is said to lie in direct line with the Prescot bypass and during construction of the bypass a tunnel was unearthed, which is thought to lead to Prescot church. Whether this could have been part of the same passageway and whether there really was a monastery on Riding Hill is a source of intriguing speculation. Whatever the truth of the matter, there is no question that over the years there have been sightings of a figure dressed in the unmistakable attire of a monk.

In the late 1970s three local men used to take a motorbike up to Riding Hill. They would ride the bike along a track through the woods which was always covered with short grass. According to legend the grass was kept short by the regular passage of monks walking over it. On one of their visits the three of them stopped for a cigarette higher up the hill and, looking down at the track, they noticed a figure glide down the path and vanish into thin air. The figure appeared to be wearing a duffle coat. Ghostly monk or not, the appearance of this mysterious apparition was disturbing enough for them to put an end to that day's motocross.

Other sightings have established the presence on Liverpool Drive of an eerie figure, which has been seen crossing the road to pass straight through a fence and then vanish.

Lonely as this figure may be wandering the paths of Knowsley, he is certainly not alone if you consider the many encounters across the country that have been related in this chapter. It would seem that many more former monks still maintain a spiritual life far beyond the grave.

Knowsley Hall

51

Friends of the Family

It would be a mistake to think that every ghost is any more sinister or frightening that a member of the family suddenly encountered in a dark corridor at night, or met by chance in an unexpected and unfamiliar place.

Many historic houses are haunted by former occupants, who held their old homes in such great affection that they have retained an interest in the future well-being of the house they loved (and frequently the people living in it). This affection has been sufficiently compelling to keep them from settling into eternal peace until they have been assured that all will be well after they have gone.

For the late Seigneur Cecil de Sausmarez, MBE, his home at **Sausmarez Manor** was his one great passion. His successor, Peter de Sausmarez, explains that he adored showing people round the house. In the winter, when the house was officially closed, Cecil could be seen at the window looking rather forlorn. Occasionally he would spot a couple of desultory people wandering about and would rush out to get into conversation with them, which invariably led to him showing them round the house on a personal tour conducted by the Seigneur himself.

At that time Peter and his family were sharing the house with Cecil and his wife. It was their home and, without the need to keep it especially tidy for visitors, they were in the habit, like most families, of leaving things lying around without having to worry too much about how the rooms looked. So Cecil's impromptu tours understandably began to annoy Peter's wife.

He was asked if he could curb his desire to show off his home and for a while he kept to his promise. But every now and then the temptation became too much and on one occasion Peter's wife was interrupted in the bathroom, where she had nipped in without locking the door, by Cecil and two rather pretty German girls, whom he was showing round the house.

'He was deaf, so she couldn't shout at him,' Peter explains. 'But it did cause quite a lot of embarrassment.' So, Cecil was taken aside and told firmly that he really had to put a stop to taking visitors through the house in the winter.

As it happened, nature intervened and Cecil's unscheduled tours came to an abrupt end when he died suddenly about a fortnight later – not that his death was wholly unexpected. As a little boy he had helped plant an elm and had been told, possibly as a joke, that he and the tree would die in the same year. Joke or not, this prediction must have stuck in his mind. So, in a way, Cecil's demise was probably hastened by the onset of Dutch Elm Disease.

A couple of weeks after his funeral, Peter and his secretary were working in their office at the top of the house when the front door opened downstairs and they heard a familiar voice delivering another personal tour. Peter was halfway down the stairs to give Cecil a piece of his mind when it dawned on him that it couldn't be the former Seigneur for the simple reason that he was dead.

Back in his office, Peter admitted rather sheepishly to his secretary, 'You know it's extraordinary. I heard a voice down there.'

'Yes, you did,' she said. 'It was Cecil.'

Portrait of the late Seigneur Cecil de Sausmarez

Dunvegan Castle

But as she said it, she also realised that it couldn't be him.

Yet it happened for a whole month. Every morning at eleven o'clock, Cecil de Sausmarez was heard extolling the delights of the home he loved so much. Then one day, his visits just stopped and his personal tours of Sausmarez Manor ended for good.

Following the death of John MacLeod of MacLeod in February 2007, his body was brought back to **Dunvegan Castle** on the Isle of Skye, for nearly 800 years the ancient home and stronghold of the Chiefs of MacLeod. The late Chief returned to Dunvegan for the last time two nights before his funeral and his coffin was placed in the Library so that the family and other mourners could pay him their respects.

On the night before his funeral Maureen Byers, the Castle Curator, dined with the family in the Dining Room next to the Library, and said goodnight to the former Chief for the last time before switching off the lights, setting the alarm system and going to bed in her own apartment on the floor below. At half-past three she was woken by the sound of the alarms going off. 'By looking at the control board I can see where the problem is – it's usually the restaurant or somewhere like that,' Maureen says. 'But when I looked, the security lights were counting down, as if the alarms had just been set.'

Thinking that one of the family may have got up and gone downstairs, she reached for the telephone, whereupon all the lights went out and she found herself in complete darkness. She heard a noise which sounded like the slamming of the boiler room door, just a few yards from her private door. With mounting anxiety she tried telephoning various numbers in and around the Castle, but none of them were working. Even her mobile phone refused to function. In the end Maureen managed to get through to someone who told her there was a power cut, which was strange because it was a very calm night.

Maureen Byers takes up the story: 'The situation with the alarm is that when we have a problem, we have a battery back-up. But that night I couldn't do anything with it; it was completely dead. So there was no security, no lights and alarm noises still going off. There was also a lot clattering going on upstairs, so I did feel very unsettled.'

Fortunately she was also able to make contact with the housekeeper, a quarter of a mile away. She had two of her grandchildren staying with her, who had arrived for the funeral the next day. They all agreed to spend the rest of the night with Maureen in her apartment, and by the time they arrived it was four o'clock in the morning.

When the housekeeper arrived Maureen suggested that they check the main security panel at the back door and that the family and guests upstairs were alright. They went to check the back door security board first. When they looked the security board was reading 'Chief John's Flat'.

Still in total darkness, Maureen and the housekeeper edged their way up to the top floor of the Castle to see what was amiss, but everybody was fast asleep and there was no sign of what had happened. So, they went back down and sat till seven o'clock, when the housekeeper usually came in to do the cleaning. Then, just before seven o'clock, when they were leaving Maureen's flat, the electricity came back on, the alarm stopped ringing and the security board returned to its default mode to read 'MacLeod Estates'.

After what Maureen Byers disarmingly refers to as 'a very strange evening' she recounted what had happened to the family and they agreed that Chief John had been completely obsessed with the heating system and the Castle alarms and when in residence he always set the alarms and turned down the heating every evening; they all felt that he was setting them for the last time as he went. 'I don't think he meant to scare me,' Maureen adds.

When the maintenance men checked the alarm system they found no fault that could explain their going off, and plumbers had to be called to mend a fault in the boiler room which left the

Fairy Flag at Dunvegan Castle

Castle without hot water for a few days. Equally strange and inexplicable was what had happened to the celebrated Fairy Flag. As Dunvegan's most treasured possession and the saviour of the MacLeods in battle on at least two occasions in the history of the clan, this had been taken down from its normal location in the Drawing Room and placed in the Library to be beside the late Chief. For no accountable reason, though, the Fairy Flag had slipped from its pedestal in the Library.

Maureen feels most strongly that on the last night before his funeral John was saying his final goodbyes. Since his funeral she has not felt his presence in the same way.

Knebworth House in Hertfordshire was transformed into a Gothic fantasy by the Victorian writer and politician Edward Bulwer-Lytton, after he inherited the family seat on the death of his mother in 1843, when he was 40 years old. For 30 years, until his death in 1873, his personality permeated the house and his presence there lasted long after his death. His successor, Lady Cobbold, writes that he makes himself known to many.

In 1973 a special exhibition was held to mark the centenary of Edward Bulwer-Lytton's death. This was set up in Knebworth's State Drawing Room, next to Bulwer-Lytton's study, and while it was in place the burglar alarm went off for several nights running at exactly two o'clock in the morning. It was the kind of alarm that is activated by movement, so a caretaker undertook to sit up all night to see what was setting it off. He was convinced that the ropes around the display panels and cases moved as if someone was walking around them and stopping to study what was on show.

'Bulwer-Lytton must have been satisfied with our efforts,' Lady Cobbold comments, 'for the problem stopped until the very last night before we took the exhibition down, when the alarm went off at two o'clock again. We decided that it was Sir Edward having a last look around his own centenary exhibition.'

A strong affection for a house is invariably combined with an equally strong interest in the family who live there, as several encounters with deceased residents confirm. In 1925 Lady Tankerville, kinswoman of the present owners, made a written record of the ghosts at **Chillingham Castle**. Among those described was a curious encounter with someone she had never expected to see.

Edward Bulwer-Lytton's Study at Knebworth

The first time I ever saw Chillingham was in the company of a so-called ghost. I had left Europe at the time, nevertheless, on waking one morning, at sunrise, I seemed to find myself there, walking through the West Lodge entrance, and along the avenue at Chillingham.

I had made the acquaintance of my future husband some months before and had no expectation of ever seeing him again. I knew nothing of his home, no one had described it to me, nor had I seen any photographs; but, finding myself there I was full of interest and curiosity and, noticing a good many details, was especially wondering why the Castle was not visible from the avenue, asking myself if it meant I should, in the flesh, never see the Castle, when a young man came forward and, introducing himself as Lord Bennet's brother (my husband's name at that time) he said, 'I have come to walk with you until George is ready.' We turned back and went towards the park, where my husband joined us and his brother disappeared. This brother had died two years before and in after years I had no difficulty in recognising his photograph. He seemed not satisfied to leave the old home without knowing of the fulfilment of his longing to see the surviving brother

married and settled down. I never saw him again; his mind was now at rest.

Over half a century later another future bride was visited by a more distant relative of her husband-to-be. During her engagement, the future Mrs Prideaux-Brune was staying at **Prideaux Place** when 'the ever-present' Lady in White wafted through the bedroom in which she was staying. Entering by the window, she passed through the room and straight into the bathroom. Interestingly, Elisabeth Prideaux-Brune felt that there was 'nothing remotely threatening about her.' It seemed that one of the ancestors was checking her out, which seemed quite natural at the time. The arrival of the 'White Lady' was preceded by a slight wind moving the curtains. The ghost followed and then vanished through the bathroom wall.

At **Isel Hall** in Cumbria it is a lady in blue who has taken to sitting on the end of a particular bed when young men are sleeping in it. Mary Burkett, who inherited the house in 1986 and who has kindly written this (only slightly edited) account of the ghost at Isel, first became aware of her spectral presence when a friend came to stay with three young cousins: a teenage boy and his two younger sisters. Thinking that the two little girls would enjoy sleeping in a four-poster bed, Miss Burkett showed them to a bedroom in the Hall's ancient Peel Tower; their elder brother was given a little bedroom down the corridor. The next day she happened to notice that her young guests had swapped rooms and casually asked her friend why. It turned out that that boy felt too embarrassed to admit that he was scared of sleeping in the room after seeing a woman in a blue dress sitting on the end of his bed. So he had discreetly asked his sisters to change rooms with him, not telling them the reason. Nothing was said and their holiday passed without further mention – but Mary Burkett remembered the remark about the 'woman in the blue dress'.

The next visitor to sleep in that room was a young man, who was to do a job pointing the walls in the sunken garden, in return for which Mary Burkett was providing him with board and lodging and a small wage. He had a healthy appetite and was working hard. One morning he did not come down to breakfast and thinking of time creeping by she went up to rouse him. She knocked and when there was no reply pushed the door open and popped her head round, to find him fast asleep but with his electric light on. He woke up and over breakfast she said she didn't mind if he turned the light off at night, but he muttered something about falling asleep reading a book and they left it at that.

Miss Burkett had not seen any book and later mentioned it to her sculptor friend, with whom her 'temporary builder' worked as an assistant. Her friend answered in confidence that he was too scared to go to sleep without the light on in case 'she' came back. He was adamant that there was a lady in a blue dress sitting on the end of his bed.

This time the story really registered. After the young builder had finished his work at Isel, Mary Burkett looked around the room and from the wooden overmantle saw the initials of a Wilfrid Lawson married to Jane who was the sixth daughter of Edward and Margaret Musgrave of Hayton Castle. Could she have been the woman in the blue dress?

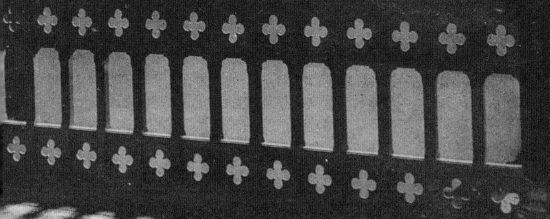

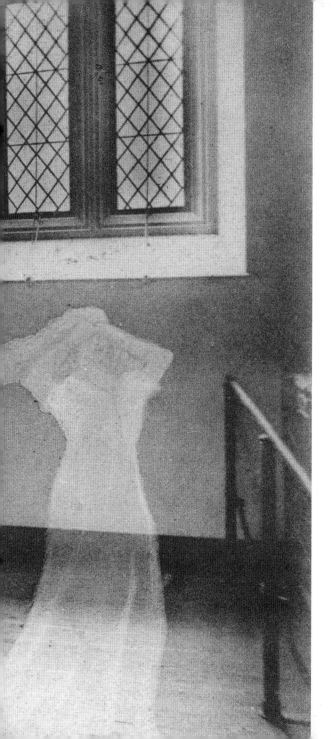

That was the second sighting of her. Number three came a year or so later.

A young friend from Windermere had been in the habit of coming up to stay and help Miss Burkett in all sorts of jobs at Isel. On one particular visit when told, 'You're in the same bedroom', to Miss Burkett's surprise he replied very firmly, 'I'm not sleeping in that bedroom again. Last time a woman in a blue dress sat on the end of my bed!'

Mary Burkett was astonished as she had been extremely careful not to mention a word about the woman to anyone at all. So he must have seen her for himself. Anyway, he didn't sleep in that room again.

That might have been the end of the story. There had been nothing but a woman sitting on the end of the bed of three young men at separate times. They'd never met each other, came from different parts of England and their hostess hadn't uttered a word to anyone about the episodes. They were themselves quite secretive, perhaps because they felt it was a bit 'unmanly' to have seen such a ghostly apparition. But then,

only a couple of years ago, there was a sequel to the whole thing.

The tree specialist at Isel Hall brought the woodman to see Miss Burkett about the felling of a wood and they sat out on the terrace to discuss it all. John, the woodman, came from Lanercost and was born at the wood yard at the saw mill of Naworth Castle; the then young Lord Carlisle was born in the Castle up the hill, at the same time, so naturally the two little boys became friends – and not just casual friends, but with a real bond, addressing each other by first names. Lord Carlisle was also a good friend of Miss Burkett's and they had known each other for years.

As she sat out on the terrace with the two men discussing the work in the wood, John turned to her and asked, 'Did Charlie ever tell you the story about the ghost?' She answered that he had not and John launched into it.

Apparently some forty years ago, when Lord Carlisle would still have been a young man (so far the woman in blue only sat on the beds of young men), he was invited to dinner with Margaret Austen Leigh, the previous owner, who had left Isel to Miss Burkett. 'I know she had long since desisted from having dinner parties,' writes Miss Burkett, 'so it must have been *at least* forty years ago.'

Lord Carlisle always liked his drink and Margaret was a good hostess; after the meal she had said to him that he couldn't drive back like that and he should therefore stay the night.

As John the woodman faithfully recounted, when the other guests had gone she had led him up to the little room and shown him the bed. Lord Carlisle had the light on but there was still light coming through the curtains because it was summer time. As he reached to extinguish the light he saw, in John's account, 'A woman in a blue silk dress, with blonde curly hair sitting on the end of my bed'.

Lord Carlisle thought she was real and said, 'Who are you? Where did you come from? Get out of my room!'

But she sat impassively smiling at him. He was even more furious and turned in his bed to grab a pillow which he hurled at her and watched it as it went right through her. She rose looking pained and walked towards the door and then right through the door.

The poor young man was terrified and despite his slightly inebriated state (though the experience may have sobered him up somewhat), he got up, dressed and drove home. By the next morning he was still in a state of terror, sought out his chum and told him the whole story. John said the memory is as vivid today as the day he was told it because of Charlie's state of intense excitement – from what had evidently been a terrifying experience for him. So to hear the story from John as relayed by Charlie – with a few additional details such as the 'silk', the 'fair curls' and the rest – and yet confirming there was a woman in a blue silk dress, added powerfully to the story and acted as an irrefutable confirmation.

'In the absence of more sightings,' Miss Burkett concludes, 'it is now frequently offered in auctions of promises: bed and breakfast in a haunted room. I believe the highest raised was £350 and no ghost buster has been lucky so far.'

The material in a lady's dress proved to be a striking detail in a ghostly encounter along the Scottish border at **Traquair House**, in Peebleshire. With a history that reaches back 900 years, Traquair is a prime candidate for ghostly goings-on, though interestingly Traquair's principal visitation dates from comparatively recently: a warm July afternoon in the 1920s to be precise.

This was when Andrew Brown, a young farmhand on the estate, was working in the joiner's shop situated just off the old avenue leading to Traquair House. The avenue, it should be said, symbolises the staunch support given by the 5th Earl of Traquair to the Jacobite cause. As he wished Godspeed to Prince Charles Edward Stuart on his march to London in 1745, the earl swore that the Bear Gates at the entrance to the avenue would remain closed until a Stuart monarch sat on the throne again. To this day the gates have remained shut and the avenue has long since grassed over.

All of this was probably far from the young farmhand's thoughts as he bent over his work. However, he set his work aside when he became aware of the sound of someone walking outside. Going to the door, he saw a woman approaching, dressed in the style of the previous century. Andrew watched in amazement as she walked straight through the little gate leading into the fenced-off area by the joiner's shop – without stopping to open it – and then through the gate on the other side and on across the avenue.

Determined to get to the bottom of his strange encounter, he contacted a friend in nearby Innerleithen, whose grandmother had been a dressmaker to Lady Louisa Stuart, sister to the last Earl of Traquair. Following her brother's death, she had lived on at Traquair House until her own death at the age of 99 in 1875. Her dressmaker had kept samples of all the materials she had used to make clothes for Lady Louisa and these had now passed to her granddaughter. Looking through them, Andrew quickly found what he was looking for – the very material of the dress worn by the mysterious lady he had seen.

Traquair House

67

From the descendant of one of her gardeners he also discovered that the old lady's regular walk had been around the avenue – at a time before the joiner's shop had been built. Though why she had visited Andrew Brown that summer afternoon remains an unresolved mystery.

Seeking to be alone from other company in the Wood Library, which lies off the Holland Library at **Woburn Abbey**, can prompt the unsettling arrival of ghostly company instead. According to the Duke of Bedford, 'No one has ever been very comfortable sitting in that room on their own.' Although he has never seen it himself, the library doors have been seen to open and close on their own and for no apparent reason; both his father and grandfather felt uncomfortable sitting in

Closed Bear Gates at Traquair House

there. It turns out that this was the favourite room of Georgiana, who was married to the 6th Duke in the early 19th century. Sensing someone by themselves in the room she loved so much during her own time at Woburn, she goes to join them – unseen but ever-present.

A former curator was working in the Wood Library one sunny day when she noticed a most beautiful rose fragrance. On looking up she found herself face to face with a lady in a rich navy blue dress, who then faded away. Later she discovered that a retired security officer had also noticed this perfume on a number of occasions and, many months later, it was found that Esprit de Rose was the favourite perfume of Georgiana.

Books attract another of Woburn's ghosts, that of one Mr Pickering, one of the previous librarians. The same curator believes that she heard him one evening in her office (which had once been his office) down in the vaults. She could hear the heavy pages of an old volume being turned in the stillness but when she spoke to the invisible reader the sound stopped.

Wood Library through the Holland Library at Woburn Abbey

The presence of former 20th-century residents is still sensed at **Kiplin Hall**, which was requisitioned by the army and then by the RAF during the Second World War. In one of the flats used by officers, two of the rooms have been preserved as they were left when hostilities ended in 1945. Many visitors to Kiplin, and some of the Hall's volunteers, on entering what was the kitchen during the war have become aware of a presence, and many have spoken of the strong smell of pipe or cigar smoke.

One evening in 2006, a team of paranormal investigators visited Kiplin. Several members of the group were filming, using infra-red video cameras. One of the girls looked away from her viewing screen and suddenly screamed, almost dropping the camera. When she had recovered herself sufficiently to speak, she told the Hall's curator that as she looked over her left shoulder, she was terrified to see a man's face peering right into hers.

Another paranormal investigator, on her first visit to Kiplin in September 2005, saw two airmen in the kitchen. One of the men was leaning on the mantel of the kitchen range, and the other standing near the door opposite, which was closed behind him. One of the men appeared to be a commanding officer, and he was arguing with the other man, apparently over something that had not gone to plan on a particular night. The investigator could smell pipe smoke, and said that there were several other younger men in the room, making tea and sitting around waiting to be called to go out for that night's mission. An officer was giving a lot of orders. It appeared that a night of great wartime activity was being relived. The investigator felt that the names 'Harris' and 'Peter' were relevant. There is a book at Kiplin signed by airmen who came in part of 1944 – it has two signatures of Harrison.

Experiences in the Second World War kitchen appear to link in to the room known, in the late 19th century, as the Bachelors' Room, where single male visitors slept to ensure the modesty of the young lady visitors. This room is now the

Second World War kitchen at Kiplin Hall

Hall's Special Exhibition Room. When the same paranormal investigator entered the room, she felt a strong military presence reporting that 'lots of soldiers left from here and returned to here'. She said that it was winter, and a commanding officer was giving a talk or briefing, standing by a roaring fire, which blazed in the fireplace.

At **Whitmore Hall**, near Newcastle-under-Lyme in Staffordshire, sounds of a different kind have become audible during the last decade, from the time when the current owner and his wife began to investigate behind the walls of their Carolingian manor house. Whitmore Hall has been the home of the Mainwarings, descendants of the original Norman owners, for over 900 years, and it has always been understood by recent generations that the attractive 17th-century brick façade was actually built over the exterior of an older house. When the house passed to Guy Cavenagh-Mainwaring and his wife in the mid-1990s, they set about investigating this and discovered the original 14th-century house still standing within the walls of their home. Two large holes were made and since then have been left

open. They also discovered something else – the sound of music filtering through these holes! On at least a dozen occasions over the last decade members of the family (except Mr Cavenagh-Mainwaring himself) and a number of friends have heard someone playing what sounds like a harpsichord in the house. Very faint and very beautiful, Whitmore's ghostly music is always heard at night at 11 o'clock. On one occasion, the Cavenagh-Mainwarings' daughter, who lives at the back of the hall with her family, heard the sounds of a party taking place downstairs at night and the sound of a woman singing. As her mother, Christine, puts it, 'It's almost as if something has been let out of the walls.'

Until 2006 the family thought they knew who the harpsichordist was. In the course of reorganising pictures in the house, the portrait of Ann Mainwaring (née Lomax) who died in 1693, had been moved upstairs to hang beside the portrait of her husband. Reunited with him after a century or more, the Cavenagh-Mainwarings thought that the music they heard was her way of saying 'thank you'.

71

However, doubt was cast on that theory when a friend of their daughter came to stay at Whitmore in 2006. She had some psychic powers and through the use of a divining rod made some startling discoveries. Having told her nothing about whom they suspected of being the ghostly musician, Christine Cavenagh-Mainwaring asked if her daughter's friend could discover who the musician was and why she had started playing for them. Their guest agreed to find out what she could and after being left to get on with it reported later in the day that the musician was a woman who had died in 1798. A quick review of the Mainwaring family history revealed that one Sarah Mainwaring (née Bunbury) had indeed died that year. Better still, her portrait was hanging in the hall – undated. So, Christine asked if her guest could identify the harpsichordist from the pictures in the house and watched in amazement as she identified Sarah Bunbury straight away.

With her identity clarified, Christine was keen to discover the reason that her predecessor had started playing music in the house. The answer, she was told, was that Sarah was so happy that the house was full of children once again; the current generation are in fact the first children to have been brought up at Whitmore Hall for 150 years. Sarah Bunbury loved children and had eight of her own. The music that sounded through the hall late at night was her expression of happiness that Whitmore Hall echoed with their voices and laughter once more.

However, one further detail remained to be divulged by Whitmore's psychic visitor. It was not a harpsichord Sarah Bunbury was playing, but a clavichord – a smaller instrument than a harpsichord, rectangular in shape. As a coda, the visitor with the divining rod was even able to show where Sarah Bunbury's clavichord used to stand.

Having established the identity of their ghostly musician, Christine Cavenagh-Mainwaring is happy to admit to going to talk to her portrait from time to time. 'I think, what a nice person,' she says. In a house as venerable as Whitmore Hall, a gap of 200 years between the two of them counts for little.

Whitmore Hall

One of the most curious ghost stories from an historic house actually tells of a harpsichord-playing occupant who was seen as a 'ghost' when he wasn't dead. The setting was **Levens Hall**, the Cumbrian home of the Bagot family. Robin Bagot, who was then living at Levens, was away on business. During his absence a friend of the family came to tea, bringing another friend with him, a priest as it happened. While they were having tea all the lights went out and were still out when the visitors left. So Mrs Bagot was rather surprised to get a telephone call a little later that day, in the course of which her tea-time guests mentioned that they were pleased that the lights had come back on again.

But they hadn't, she told him; the electricity at Levens was still off. Before leaving, the priest said he had popped upstairs to see someone who was unwell in bed and on his way he had come across a man sitting in the corner of a room playing the harpsichord.

'But that's impossible,' Mrs Bagot told him. 'Robin's away and he's the only one who plays it.'

So the priest came back the next day and Robin Bagot sat at the harpsichord and played his favourite tune. To everyone's bemusement, the priest confirmed that that was the music he had heard the previous afternoon and that Robin Bagot was the musician he had seen sitting at the keyboard playing it. Hal Bagot, Robin's son and his wife, Susan still have the letter the priest wrote confirming the details of his very strange experience at Levens.

Levens Hall is also the home to the ghost of a little black dog which has been seen with various members of the family. Susan Bagot was once seen with it when she was walking in the grounds in front of the house with one of the family labradors, although neither she nor her own dog were aware of their ghostly four-footed companion. It was only when a visitor was speaking to her later that the presence of the little black dog was referred to. There was no mistaking who had been seen either; the visitor was able to describe precisely what Mrs Bagot had been wearing at the time and the labrador she had been walking with.

The little black dog, which has been spotted inside the house at times, was equally attentive to her mother-in-law. On one occasion she had been out walking when a friend drove by and stopped to offer her lift. Mrs Bagot senior accepted and got in, only to be asked by the driver, 'What about your dog?'

'I haven't got a dog,' she answered, somewhat mystified. Presumably her spectral companion found its own way back to Levens Hall.

Although **Ballindalloch Castle** is home to a retinue of small dogs, they are all cheerfully of this world and enjoying life to the full in their matchless home on the eastern side of the Highlands in the glorious Spey Valley in Banffshire. However, Ballindalloch has supernatural beings of the human variety who are equally attached to the Castle and the Macpherson-Grant family, who have lived there since the 16th century. General James Grant is still making spectral forays up and down the passages, always dressed in a kilt and always carrying a bottle of whisky to offer a dram to anyone going by, though no one ever takes it. As one of the most celebrated *bon viveurs* of his day, he was a lively and hospitable host – as he appears to be long after his death.

The current Laird of Ballindalloch, Mrs Clare Macpherson-Grant Russell, is equally welcoming to the many and varied guests who come to her family's ancient home to enjoy the best of

General James Grant

Ballindalloch Castle

Highland hospitality and field sports. Although she has not seen her illustrious forebear wandering the passages of the home they both love, it hasn't escaped her that those who do see ghosts, always see the same two at Ballindalloch.

General Grant is one, of course. The other is a beautiful lady in a pink crinoline dress who is always encountered in the Pink Tower bedroom. She has been remarked on by a good number of visitors down the years, but it was one who got into conversation with Mrs Russell that shed more light on her.

'She was one of your relations who lived in the 18th century,' he explained, 'and she lost a beloved child of five years old. And when you, Mrs Russell, came to the Castle as a child of five [a fact which was not referred to anywhere in visitor material at Ballindalloch at the time] she thought you were her long-lost child. You don't know this, Mrs Russell, but you have nearly died three times in your life and three times she has saved you. She is, in fact, your guardian angel and will guard you and your family forever. So, please have happy thoughts when you go into that room.'

'I felt goose pimply all over,' Mrs Russell says. 'And you start wondering to yourself, does he go round every house telling that to people? Then, of course, I started thinking when I nearly died. I was once nearly killed by a mad Russian out shooting; I've still got the holes in my coat.

'I always remember arriving at a car crash literally as it happened. That day I had gone back to collect my scarf, because it was raining. If it hadn't it would have been me in the crash. So maybe that was it.

'The extraordinary thing is that I remember my mother and I talking about ghosts long before we knew anything abut the Pink Lady. I asked my mother, if there was a haunted room in the Castle, which one did she think it would be? And we both came up with that room.

'Occasionally our dogs will go in there and bark, and something I was told only recently was that a child of five years had died in that room.'

According to legend supernatural forces have been at work taking care of Ballindalloch and its occupants since the earliest days of the Castle. On the hill above it the foundations of a Z-shaped structure can be seen, where, it is said, building the first castle began. But every night the masons' efforts were blown down until the laird of the day rode up to find out what was going on. Overlooking the builders' fruitless efforts scattered around him, he heard a mysterious voice telling him, 'Build it in the coo-haugh [the cow meadow].' The laird followed this advice and moved the construction site down into the valley below, where Ballindalloch Castle has been

Pink Tower bedroom at Ballindalloch Castle

The impaling spike in the Torture Chamber at Chillingham Castle

standing safe and secure since the middle of the 16th century.

One of the most compelling examples of benevolent spirits at work comes from **Chillingham Castle**, where Sir Humphry Wakefield has been tirelessly at work to restore this ancient fortress. Chillingham, like many castles either side of the Scottish border, has a violent and gruesome history. The Castle has its own grim dungeon where the walls are etched with the pathetic 'diary' scratchings and initials of those once incarcerated there, and a torture chamber for good measure. The latter is still equipped with a ghastly array of instruments of torment: a stretcher rack, a nailed barrel in which victims were rolled while the flesh was shredded from their bodies, a spiked chair and an impaling spike on which victims suffered the most appallingly slow and excruciating death. Little wonder that Chillingham has acquired the reputation of being England's most haunted castle.

It's little wonder too that when Sir Humphry Wakefield first arrived there he felt as if he was 'walking through shadows'. His sense that the

Castle had an overwhelming atmosphere of malign memories was confirmed by a priest who came to stay. There was such a strong presence at Chillingham, the priest explained, he felt quite incapable of doing anything about it. The priest left; Sir Humphry Wakefield did not. And when his priest friend returned five years later the change he sensed was astounding. The presence was as strong as before, he explained, but this time the atmosphere was one of wholly benign support. 'The spirits are all punting for you like mad,' he told his host. 'They all think you're wonderful.'

So what had brought about this remarkable change? Put simply, it was a growing affection for and an unflinching commitment to Chillingham Castle, which had been in dire need of restoration – a task which Sir Humphry had tackled with energy and no shortage of personal toil. Here, at least, his efforts did not pass without notice or attention; the spirits were backing him from the outset.

On one occasion, when he was up a ladder tackling a badly decayed window, the masonry came away in his hands and he was sent tumbling to the rubble-strewn ground below. Whoever, or whatever, was guiding him, directed his fall onto a bale of straw ten feet from the foot of the ladder and he emerged unscathed. Similarly, the only time when he wore a hard hat was the time when another large piece of stone broke free from the walls and ricocheted off his providently protected head.

For his part, Sir Humphry was persuaded to buy, unseen, 'a curiously carved stone weighing 1¼ tons' to spare it from being broken up. Only when it was delivered did he discover that it was a 17th-century carving of the Chillingham Castle coat of arms.

While in New York, he was stopped by a gypsy on Madison Avenue, who told him that he lived in a haunted house, but that the spirits wished him well. When a Maori girl visited Chillingham she showed great interest in talking to the ghosts and reported back that the Chillingham ghosts thought the castle 'Ghost Tour' was 'the funniest cabaret they had ever heard'.

Other Polynesian visitors to Chillingham, from Vanuatu this time, showed the same respect for, and ability to communicate with, the spirit world – human and natural. Some forestry work was planned at Chillingham when they visited. Through a translator they conveyed a message from the trees, who asked not be cut down, but to be allowed to fall down, rest there and be reborn in their children; nor did they want to be planted out in the fields as they liked 'chatting to each other'. Lyrical, whimsical, as it may appear, this is increasingly becoming accepted forestry practice now, and the Chillingham trees are allowed to remain growing close to each other to reach the end they desired.

Whatever changes Sir Humphry instigated at Chillingham Castle were neatly summed up by the daughter of the previous owner who told him on a return visit after a long absence that he had 'removed evil from the place' – the great point of the Castle in her view!

As in many other historic houses, the spiritual friends of the family approve and applaud him and show their appreciation as only they can; if nothing more, the ghosts of Chillingham Castle attract a growing number of visitors every year.

Unquiet Graves

Ghosts may manifest themselves in a variety of forms but the traditional conception of a ghost is that of a restless spirit forced by fate to wander abroad like the ghost of Hamlet's father, unable to find lasting peace in the world that lies beyond the grave.

Britain's historic houses are richly populated with the spirits of those who passed into death as a result of violence, or still carrying with them the trauma of some devastating event that shrouded their life on earth. A good number of these female spirits take the form of a 'White Lady' or a 'Grey Lady' who has appeared sufficiently often for her to become part of the folklore and tradition of the house.

Among the most haunted buildings in Britain is **Samlesbury Hall**, near Preston in Lancashire, which is haunted by a celebrated White Lady, the ghost of Lady Dorothy Southworth. The Southworths were a Roman Catholic family who

cleaved to their faith during the years of Tudor persecution. The Priest's Room in the Hall is so named after a Catholic priest was murdered there during the Reformation. More chilling is the fact that the stains of blood left by his bleeding body refuse to go away. One owner of the house tried to get rid of them by ripping up the floor and replacing it with a fresh one, only to find the ghastly red marks continuing to appear, no matter what he did to remove them.

Dorothy's own story is no less shocking. She suffered the misfortune of falling in love with a Protestant soldier at a time when tensions between the two faiths were at their most

Samlesbury Hall

extreme. Her father forbade her from her seeing her beloved, a member of the De Houghton family, ever again. But young love was too strong to be curbed by parental threats and the lovers planned to elope. On the night of their planned escape, De Houghton came to Samlesbury Hall with two friends to collect Dorothy. But instead of the girl he was hoping to marry, they were met by her brothers, who set upon the three young men and killed them; their bodies were buried near the outer poles of the house drawbridge.

Poor Dorothy had witnessed this outrage and was packed off to France to spend the rest of her life in a convent. Here, fate kindly granted her an early release as she soon died of a broken heart. However, her ghost has never left Samlesbury Hall where she has been seen on many occasions. Visitors have reported seeing the White Lady on the driveway to the Hall; when she has turned towards them, they have turned and run away. A lady dressed in white has flagged down buses and taxis, but has disappeared when they have stopped to let her in. Even a police patrol car is said to have collided with a figure dressed in white, but when the shaken officers got out to investigate what had happened there was no one to be seen, nor did their vehicle show any signs of damage.

Perhaps the most poignant encounters are those concerning soldiers, for Dorothy's lover, De Houghton, was a soldier. During the 1920s two soldiers of a regiment stationed at Samlesbury Hall reported being followed by the White Lady. One was said to be so terrified by the experience that he never recovered. During the Second World War, when Samlesbury again hosted many soldiers, there were numerous sightings of the White Lady, who was presumably searching among them in the vain hope of finding her lost love.

The White Lady of **Muncaster Castle** haunts the Castle gardens and part of the main road, where she has been seen quite often. Her presence took on particular significance after two people, who had seen her on separate occasions, were interviewed by the university professor who for a good many years has been carrying out investigations into paranormal activities at Muncaster. 'I was amazed,' says Peter Frost-Pennington, whose family live in the Castle today, 'because their stories were significantly different, but it was obviously the same phenomenon they were seeing. It was really spooky for me to realise that these people had thought that they had seen something perfectly normal. It was only afterwards that they realised that what they were describing to others was in fact the fabled ghost of the White Lady of Muncaster Castle.'

This experience prompted Peter to investigate for himself and he discovered that at some time in the 19th century a poor servant girl had been murdered or otherwise done away with and her death had been made to look like suicide. However, repeated attempts to hide her body failed and she kept reappearing. At the same time the inquest papers hint at attempts to cover up some skulduggery surrounding her death. As a result, her spirit has stalked the area around Muncaster Castle and at least one witness reports having seen her quite recently.

Not too far away, **Levens Hall** is haunted by one of several Grey Ladies that are seen in and around historic houses in various parts of the country. The one at Levens has been sighted by members of the family and visitors on the back drive to the house and on the bottom drive by the river. Susan Bagot, the wife of the present owner, spotted the Grey Lady while she was driving near Levens. Ahead of her, she caught sight of a figure walking along the verge, fully expecting to draw close to whoever it was when her car emerged from an approaching dip in the road. On pulling out of this, though, she looked about and saw no one. The figure she had clearly seen moments before had vanished completely.

Mrs Bagot's mother saw the Grey Lady on at least two occasions before mentioning it to her daughter and son-in-law. On one sighting she too had been driving into the Hall on the bottom drive when she noticed 'a lady, rather poorly dressed in a long grey dress, with her hair in a bun' walking in front of her. Her second encounter was equally strong. But being, in her daughter's words, 'an extremely straightforward Scot', she had said nothing about what she had seen, assuming that she would be dismissed by the family as just a fey old woman. As far as Susan Bagot is concerned, there was no reason for her mother to have invented this story; to her the sighting of the ghostly Grey Lady was as real as seeing a living member of the family.

When it comes to pinpointing who she might be, there is a legend at Levens that a poor woman, possibly a gypsy, came begging at the front door of the Hall one bitterly cold winter night. She was refused entry and was sent round the back to the kitchen quarters. Close to death, however, she expired before getting there. In her dying breath she is said to have laid a curse on the house that no male heir would inherit Levens Hall until the River Kent ceased to flow and a white fawn was born in the Park.

Cursed, or not, this is exactly what transpired. For several generations from around 1720 Levens passed through the female line of the family until Alan Bagot was born during the icy winter of 1896, when the River Kent had frozen over and

Levens Hall

effectively ceased to flow and when a white fawn had also been born in the Park. Curiously the three male heirs to Levens since Alan Bagot have all been born in freezing weather.

Princess Marie Louise of Schleswig-Holstein was one of several visitors to **Chavenage House** who received the attention of a Grey Lady there (who may also have been responsible for blighting the male line of its residents). The princess was unaware of the incident herself, resting as she was before dinner, but her maid in the adjoining room had seen everything that passed. She was sewing, while her mistress closed her eyes, and saw 'a lady in an old-world dress' walk through her room into the one where the princess was lying on her bed. As she watched, the Grey Lady bent over Princess Marie Louise and then withdrew, fading away as she went. The princess was wholly unaware of her strange visitor, but her maid had spotted every detail. She remembered particularly her very beautiful hands and the lace ruffles she wore at her wrists.

This revelation led Princess Marie Louise to speculate whether the Grey Lady might have been related to Colonel Nathaniel Stephens, the owner of Chavenage at the time of the execution of King Charles I (she suggests it might have been the sister of Colonel Stephens, though later historians opt for his daughter Abigail). These were troubled times for the country and for Chavenage, so it comes as little surprise that the Grey Lady should still be seeking eternal rest centuries after her death.

During the Civil War, Colonel Stephens had commanded a regiment of horse and was highly regarded by Oliver Cromwell, to whom he was related through the female side of the family. Cromwell urged his kinsman to support the execution of the king in order to snuff out lingering Royalist support. Known to be a mild man, Colonel Stephens was also leader of the more moderate wing of the Roundhead faction in Parliament and he had little enthusiasm for killing his king. Only after prolonged persuasion did he reluctantly agree to support this act of regicide. The story goes that Abigail had been spending New Year elsewhere and returned to Chavenage to be met with the shocking news of what her father had agreed to. She was furious with him for bringing the family name into disrepute and foresaw an awful doom for him and his successors. Not long after the Colonel returned from London, where Charles I had been beheaded in January 1649, he was taken ill, retired to his bed and died a few months later. As the Colonel neared his final hour, relatives were summoned to his bedside to pay their

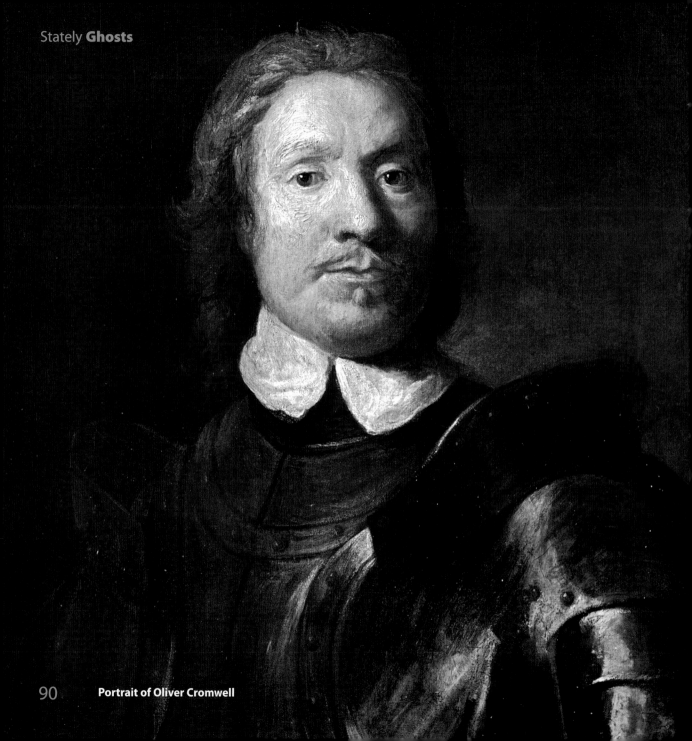

Portrait of Oliver Cromwell

last respects and, as it transpired, witness his dramatic passage into the next world.

Dead and wrapped in his shroud, the Colonel's body was ready for its final journey when a fine coach, drawn by black horses, was seen to draw up silently at the entrance. Pausing there briefly, the door of the coach was opened by an invisible force and the Colonel's body glided inside. Moving as silently as it had arrived, the coach pulled swiftly away but not before the astonished on-lookers had caught sight of the driver, a headless man dressed in royal vestments and wearing the star and regalia of the Order of the Garter. The assembled company watched it reach the gate to the manor where the coach and those riding in it burst into flames and disappeared.

The old tale, in which these strange events are related, concludes, 'The story further maintains that to this very day, every Lord of Chavenage dying in the manor house takes his departure in this ominous conveyance.' Princess Marie Louise's Grey Lady, it seems, may have achieved more than she bargained for.

As befits one of the most celebrated haunted houses in Britain, a third Grey Lady has been seen in the Chapel at **Glamis Castle** (home to the late Queen Elizabeth the Queen Mother in her younger days, when she was the Lady Elizabeth Bowes Lyon). This Grey Lady is thought to be the ghost of Janet Douglas, wife to the 6th Lord Glamis, at the time of King James V. James V had a deep loathing for the Douglas family and outlawed and exiled the whole brood of them. Janet did not leave Scotland, though, opting to help her exiled brothers from Glamis. When her husband died, the vindictive king seized the chance to imprison her in Edinburgh Castle, where she was incarcerated with her second husband and her two sons. A trumped-up charge of witchcraft was brought against her and two juries refused to sit to hear it, knowing it to be wholly false. Eventually the wicked king found a jury that would do his bidding and Janet Douglas was duly convicted and burnt at the stake the same afternoon. Her husband died trying to escape and her younger son perished in captivity. Her older son did survive, though, and when Mary Queen of Scots ascended the throne, Glamis was restored to him and his mother's spirit lingers there still.

Most often seen in the Chapel, the ghost of Janet Douglas has been spotted at prayer and occupying a chair in one corner of the back row – a chair that mysteriously remains empty even when the chapel is well filled with people; there is something about it that keeps them away.

Lady Grey (as opposed to a Grey Lady) and Mary Queen of Scots feature in two of the ghost stories from **Chillingham Castle**, both of which are connected with pictures there.

Before marrying Ford, Lord Grey of Wark and Chillingham and Earl of Tankerville, Lady Grey had been born Lady Mary Berkley. Hers was not a happy marriage and her baby daughter was still in her infancy when her husband deserted them both and ran away with his wife's sister, Lady Henrietta Berkley, for whom the Earl had built Uppark, now the property of the National Trust. The scandal and subsequent court case failed to bring him home and the poor woman was left in her dark lonely castle, with only her daughter to keep her company. One of her successors, Leonora Countess of Tankerville wrote that 'the rustle of her dress is sometimes heard along the corridors and stairs and as the disappointed and anxious wraith passes by, a chill, as of cold air, seems to seep through one's very marrow'.

Lady Grey's ceaseless search for her errant husband led her from time to time to step out of her portrait at Chillingham to go in search of him. This remarkable event was seen by a number of occupants of the Castle down the years until the picture was sold in the 1930s. The story does not end there, however.

By an extraordinary turn of events, after acquiring the Castle in recent times, Sir Humphry Wakefield chanced on the very same painting in a catalogue of paintings scheduled to be auctioned at Christie's in London. Unable to attend the auction in person, he left a high price on the portrait, confident that the picture would be his. But fate was against him, as it proved to be throughout this strange saga. The auctioneer twice forgot, or overlooked, his clearly written

Glamis Castle

bids (which had been formally confirmed) and the painting of Lady Grey went under the hammer to another bidder. Furious at this oversight, Sir Humphry managed to track down the picture's new owner, a fine art dealer, only to discover that he had just sold the painting to a collector in Australia and that Lady Grey was on her way to the opposite side of the world. At this he gave up, realising that Lady Grey had done her level best to make sure that her portrait at least was kept as far away from Chillingham Castle and its sad memories as was possible.

When he moved into the Castle, Sir Humphry brought with him a portrait of a beautiful Elizabethan lady, which had become particular favourite of his. He decided to hang this in the New Dining Room, one of a suite of rooms that had been built to welcome King James VI of Scotland, James I of England, when he came to stay at Chillingham early in the 17th century. So he was understandably disappointed – and more than a little annoyed with himself – when he found the picture on the floor the next morning, having fallen from its seemingly secure mounting on the wall; the painting was unharmed, but the frame was damaged. When this was repaired, Sir Humphry replaced the picture on a secure hook only to find it on the floor a second time the next day. To ensure it stayed put once and for all, he drove a stout nail into the wall and hung the picture on very strong wire, wound round the nail to be certain that the picture could not budge. But even this was to no avail. The next day he found his much beloved picture on the floor once again and the wire he had laboriously used to hold it in place 'shattered' – he has it still as a memento of this bizarre episode. Convinced that there was no alternative but to hang the picture somewhere else, he moved his Elizabethan lady to another part of the Castle, where she has hung undisturbed ever since.

Some time later he was visiting Longleat, which had been his grandmother's home, when he happened upon another portrait of his beautiful Elizabethan lady, identified in the catalogue of Longleat paintings as Lady Arabella Stewart. Eager to find out more about her, Sir Humphry began looking into her life as soon as he returned to

**Portrait of Lady
Arabella Stewart**

Chillingham and discovered not only who she was but also why her painting may have been so reluctant to hang where he had first put it.

It turned out that Lady Arabella Stewart was the niece of Henry Stewart, Lord Darnley, the second husband of Mary Queen of Scots with whom he had enjoyed an uneasy marriage; in fact there were suspicions that she might have had foreknowledge of the violent explosion in which he was murdered. For that reason alone there would have been little love lost between the two women – but there was more to come. They were also rivals for the throne of England.

With this degree of animosity, it is safe to presume that the last person Lady Arabella Stewart would have wanted to spend any time with would have been Mary Queen of Scots. Yet, over the chimneypiece in the New Dining Room hangs a large portrait of that very lady, Mary Queen of Scots herself.

'Manipulated by the fates', as Sir Humphry Wakefield puts it, there appeared to be no chance that their portraits could be hung in the same room without

some disturbance arising from it. Moving one of the pictures had been by far the simplest solution, and she has hung happily ever since.

Longleat House is the setting for other anxious searches undertaken by a ghostly lady: Louisa Carteret, who was married to the 2nd Viscount Weymouth in the early 18th century and who is said to walk the top floor at Longleat looking for a favourite footman who was murdered in the house.

Young, beautiful and blessed with a sweet disposition, Louisa contrasted sharply with her ill-tempered and intemperate husband, who adored her none the less. The couple had been married little more than a year when tragedy struck. Envious jostling for favour and position in a household of that size may have led one of the servants to hint to his lordship that her ladyship's personal footman may have become closer to his wife than was appropriate or desirable.

The present Marquess of Bath questions the idea that the lady of the house and the footman were lovers, while accepting that her husband could

Portrait of Louisa Carteret

easily have been persuaded that they were. In his fury and jealousy his predecessor had the footman ambushed as he left the Old Library and then thrown down the spiral staircase leading to the floor below. Not surprisingly the man reached the bottom of the staircase dead, with a broken neck.

Faced with the prospect of a murder enquiry in which the 2nd Viscount would surely be implicated, the footman's body was quickly buried beneath flagstones on the ground floor and the story was put about that he had decided to disappear. This explanation did not deceive Louisa for one, who died following the birth of her third son on Christmas Day 1736.

Her husband then opted to leave Longleat himself and set up home in the nearby village of Horningsham, with rumours circulating even then that he had been driven from the house by his late wife's ghost searching for her lost servant. Whether or not he feared her retribution from beyond the grave, the 2nd Viscount kept away from Longleat for the rest of his life.

An interesting postscript to the story came to light early in the 20th century when central heating was being plumbed in at Longleat for the first time, by the 5th Marquess. In order to install the boiler, the cellar floors had to be lowered and during the course of the excavations a decayed human body was discovered beneath some of the raised flagstones. Around it remained enough clothing to identify the corpse as that of a man dressed in the raiment and boots of the style worn by footmen in the first half of the 18th century.

These pathetic remains were hastily gathered up and buried in the local cemetery, the same cemetery where the murdered footman's master, Louisa Carteret's husband, had been laid to rest two centuries earlier.

An equally grim discovery was made at **Eyam Hall** in the late 1700s, when James Farewell Wright and his wife Jane decided to modernise the house. At that time the principal fireplace was a much bigger affair, about twice the width of the present fireplace and James decided that a smaller fireplace would be both fashionable and more economical. Whilst building work was being carried out the workmen discovered that the wall to the left of the fireplace sounded hollow and decided to investigate. They found a small room or recess and, in opening it up, recoiled in horror as a skeleton of a man was revealed. James was quickly called and, being less superstitious than the workmen, investigated further. The remains of the man's clothing suggested an earlier period and his hat, which was well preserved, was distinctly Jacobean in style. James found a notebook obviously belonging to the man and upon deciphering its contents the mystery was explained.

The skeleton was that of Sir William Vincent, who was a commander in the army of King Charles I. At the time of the Civil War, there was a much smaller building on the site of the present-day house at Eyam, which was occupied by a family of Royalist sympathisers called Edwards. In July 1644, Sir William, fleeing from the disastrous defeat at the Battle of Marston Moor, arrived at the Edwards' house seeking shelter. Knowing there were Roundheads in the area and that many of their neighbours were Parliamentary sympathisers, the Edwards were much alarmed. Although they could not refuse their guest shelter, after he had been supplied with a good meal, they suggested that he conceal himself in the secret room by the fireplace. Unfortunately for Sir William the room could only be opened from the outside. Later that night, as the Edwards had feared, Roundhead troopers arrived, tipped off by the family's neighbours. They searched the house but found nothing, and eventually, furious at having been thwarted, arrested both the Edwards and carted them off to prison to await trial. This much Sir William overheard from his hiding place and recorded in his notebook. Alas for the poor fellow, the Edwards never returned. There is no record of what happened to them. Sir William's entries in his notebook became more and more desperate but ceased after two days, when either his candle or ink gave out, or he slipped into oblivion.

Even after all these years, at the dead of night, one can still hear the spirit of the dead man knocking despairingly to be let out of the hiding place that became his tomb.

A century later Eyam Hall was the setting for another untimely death, which led to the wanderings of another distraught ghost. In the 1770s, when Major John Wright was living there, one of the servants at Eyam Hall was a young girl named Sarah, who was equally devoted to a young man she was courting in the village, and to the Major's little dog, Rags.

One day Sarah disappeared and, after a thorough search of the house and village, was nowhere to be found. However, when Rags was discovered howling beside the well in the washhouse, the Major ordered one of the servants to be lowered down the well on the bucket. To his horror the man found Sarah drowned in the water at the bottom. Her body was brought to the surface and, to enable her to have a Christian burial, her death was recorded as an accident. Nobody knew what had really happened. Did she fall? Was she pushed or did she jump? The truth is buried with her in the grave, but if the night bell is rung at the dead of night, Sarah's ghostly apparition still appears walking from the maids' bedroom to answer it. Dressed in her nightgown with a shawl and mobcap, she carries a candlestick and appears briefly uttering a heart-rending sigh before fading away.

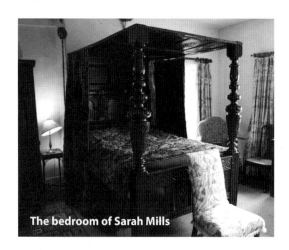

The bedroom of Sarah Mills

The sad fate of a young servant accounts for one of the ghosts at **Glamis Castle**. This was a young page-boy, who was instructed to sit on a stone bench in what is now the Queen Mother's Sitting Room and wait for further orders. Sadly, everyone forgot about him and he sat there dutifully until the cold seeped so deep into his frail body that he died. Being a small boy, however, he has lost none of his mischievous behaviour over the centuries and he is believed to get his own back

Bramall Hall

by tripping people up as they go down the step next to his bench.

Bramall Hall near Stockport is also haunted by the ghost of a former servant. Tradition holds that she was half-murdered by a member of the Davenport family, who lived at Bramall at the time. This attack took place in a bedroom in the north wing of the house, from where the poor victim was dragged, screaming, to a small room in the gable of the east front to be finally despatched.

During its eventful history Bramall Hall has become no stranger to violent and mysterious deaths. In addition to the murdered servant girl, the Hall is the setting for a celebrated legend about a ghostly Red Rider, which was recorded in ballad form by John Leigh in the late 19th century. The legend holds that during a howling storm one night the sound of horse's hooves could be heard approaching Bramall Hall. The clanging of the bell at the portal gate admitted a strange rider clad in crimson, astride a coal-black horse with eyes that shone with an unearthly glare bearing a sinister message. In spite of this, the master of the house welcomes his mysterious guest and offers sustenance and shelter. The following morning the storm has passed and the sun is rising peacefully in the bright clear sky, though all is not well in the Hall. As the ballad relates:

But the stranger's horse was nowhere seen,
And the stranger himself had fled;
And stretched on his couch, with peaceful mien,
The good old knight lay dead.

A good tale as this may be, the events described were dramatically enacted one stormy night less than a century ago. At that time Bramall Hall was owned by John Davies, a successful businessman in the brewery trade in and around Manchester. He had been master of the Hall for only two years when he fell gravely ill. Fearing the worst and not wishing to encumber his wife with the large estate he had recently acquired, including an old house likely to be full of sad memories, he moved to Llandudno, on the pretext that he would benefit from a change of air.

That year the autumn gales on the coast of north Wales were particularly violent and the one that blew up on the evening of 24 October 1927 was among the worst. It was a wild night inland at Bramall Hall as well and during his regular evening telephone call to his employers, the butler at Bramall related how he and the rest of the staff had heard the sound of a horse's hooves outside in the courtyard. The butler had made his way to the main door to see who had ridden to Bramall through so stormy a night, only to find that the stout door had opened of its own accord. As he closed it, the butler heard the horse's hooves fading away in the distance. The storm intensified, blowing down a great oak in the Park, while in his house in Llandudno John Davies breathed his last and left this life. At the time of his death neither he nor the family knew of the legend of the Red Rider.

It was the love of another new family home, one that was still under construction as it happened, that led the ghost of Anne Griffiths to haunt **Burton Agnes Hall** near Driffield in Yorkshire. Anne was the youngest of three daughters of the Hall's owner, Sir Henry Griffiths, who began building his magnificent Elizabethan house early in the 17th century. She was so excited watching her new home grow around her that she could think and talk of little else. Building

Burton Agnes Hall

work was close to completion when Anne went one afternoon to visit friends a short distance away, but while she was out she was set upon by vagabonds, attracted possibly by a fine ring she was wearing on her finger. The poor young woman was so badly beaten that when she was found and brought back to her father's house, her family could see that she had not long to live in this world.

In the few days that were left to her, Anne moved in and out of delirium. When she was lucid, though, she told her sisters she knew she would never see the house completed, which she regretted more than they could imagine. She fervently wanted to be a part of it, she told them, and asked them to preserve some part of her body in the house after her death. But when she died a day or two later, the family ignored her request and her body was buried in the churchyard intact.

Far from having been laid to rest, Anne's spirit made its presence felt immediately. Burton Agnes

Hall was filled with ghostly screams, slamming doors and the sound of someone running up and down the corridors. When her sisters remembered Anne's dying wish, the vicar was persuaded to allow her grave to be opened, so that her skull could be removed and placed in the Hall. Her wish fulfilled, Anne's ghost was at peace and as long as the skull remained in the house it caused no further trouble.

Time passed, new generations came and went in the house Sir Henry Griffiths had built and during one spring clean many years later, a dusty skull was found in a cupboard and thrown onto a rubbish cart to be taken away. Even before the cart could be moved, the house was once more filled with ghostly cries and infernal banging and crashing. The skull was quickly retrieved, brought back into the hall and this time was built into a secret alcove in one of the walls, where it has remained ever since. No one knows where in the house it is, but as long as the skull of Anne Griffiths remains securely in its resting place, her spirit is at peace and Burton Agnes Hall remains undisturbed.

Simon Cunliffe-Lister, whose family own the Hall now, explains that 'There are words of caution: that you shouldn't mock Anne or laugh at her, especially when you are upstairs as she may push you down the final flight of stairs. And if you are doing building work close to where her skull might be, things may not work out as you would want them to.'

This old story took on an interesting gloss not many years ago, which throws another interpretation on the time-honoured tale. A school party visiting the Hall were in the Queen's Bedroom, which is one of the rooms that is believed to be haunted, when one of the children aged no more than nine told a teacher that they felt unwell, had a sore head and needed to be taken outside. One of the teachers did as the child asked and, as they were coming down the stairs, the teacher was taken aback to hear the child cry out, 'My head's in a vice! My head's in a vice. Anne was murdered by her father because she was having an affair with a married man.'

Everyone accepted that this was a very strange statement for a nine-year-old to come out with unprompted and it set people thinking. Anne's father was a man of considerable power with influence on both the local and national stage. High Sherriff of the area, he was also a member of Queen Elizabeth's Council of the North. Any suggestion that a daughter of his was carrying on with a married man could have been potentially very damaging to his reputation, his standing and the fortune he was amassing. It poses the question of whether the vagabonds who attacked Anne had been deliberately sent to waylay her when she was riding out to meet her lover.

For the moment, her fate remains a mystery. As far as Simon Cunliffe-Lister is concerned, Anne (or Nancy as she has been called by staff at Burton Agnes Hall through the ages) is a happy ghost. If she makes her presence felt at all, it is by means of a strong smell of violets and lavender that people come across by chance. Like the ghosts in many historic houses, the spirit of Anne Griffiths is a figure of curiosity rather than fear. 'I would be quite interested to meet her,' Simon Cunliffe-Lister concludes.

Portrait of Anne Griffiths

Things That Go Bump in the **Night**

While ghost sightings are understandably the most graphic encounters people experience with supernatural phenomena, they do not have a monopoly over hauntings and other 'ghostly' goings-on.

Unseen, but by no means unheard, poltergeists and other eerie elements of the spirit world inhabit many historic houses up and down the country, unnerving visitors and occasionally even the owners with 'things that go bump in the night' (and during the daytime as well on occasions).

At **Dunvegan Castle** some unseen spirit was bold enough to tangle with the 28th Chief of the Clan MacLeod, Dame Flora MacLeod of MacLeod. Both she and Joan Wolridge Gordon (mother of the late Chief John) felt themselves being jostled and pushed to one side as they were going to the Castle dungeon. On another occasion, while showing a film crew through the Castle the same situation arose. When Dame Flora explained to her visitors what had happened, they all retreated to the far end of the corridor.

Maureen Byers, who has lived at Dunvegan for over ten years, on her own for most of the time, experienced something very similar a couple of years ago. Walking through Chief John's kitchen one afternoon, thinking about nothing in particular, she heard a sound which she can only describe as 'a loud and deep sigh very close to my ear'. This gave her such a fright that she felt very irritated and pushed the kitchen door open and shut

Tower Room, Ripley Castle

several times to check if she could repeat the noise and hence explain its source – but the door refused to cooperate and no similar noise emerged.

Maureen did not mention what had happened to anyone and she would probably have forgotten the incident but for what happened two months later. Walking down a corridor in the Castle one night to collect some keys the same thing happened again. This time, perhaps because it had happened in the dark and in a different part of the Castle she retreated to the security of her flat, leaving the keys to be fetched another time. If it happened a third time, she decided, she would mention it to the family because, as she says 'it was not a pleasant experience'. Fortunately for her it has not been repeated since.

In the late 1930s a poltergeist caused considerable upheaval in the Tower Room, on the first floor of the Tudor Tower at **Ripley Castle**. During alterations to the room a large fireplace was discovered behind the panelling: the workmen left for the night and the room was secured. When they entered the room the

following day the furniture was strewn all over the floor, paintings had been turned face to the wall and the clock face had been removed from a grandfather clock.

Glamis Castle has sounds that very definitely go bump in the night. In fact, legend holds, the noises were so loud and so disturbing that the room in which they occurred was sealed off from the rest of the castle for ever and the door leading to it filled in with stonework to prevent the cause of the disturbance from ever escaping.

The so-called Crypt at Glamis is one of the oldest, strongest and most impregnable parts of the original medieval fortress. Its walls are so thick that hidden within them lies the secret chamber where these alarming sounds originated. The story goes – and several versions have evolved over the centuries – that two men (some say the Lord Glamis of the day and Earl 'Beardie' Crawford) played cards in this room on a Saturday night. Despite warnings from servants, they carried on past midnight and into the small hours of Sunday morning – the day dedicated to the Lord, when games of any kind, card games in particular, were regarded as sacrilegious. As the hours ticked by and the pair remained absorbed in their cards they were joined at the table by a third player – the Devil himself. This was when the rumpus began. Such were the noises and disturbances that followed that in the end the room was sealed up (some say that the Devil himself walled them inside). Either way, it was a thorough job because the window was blocked up too; it can be seen

from the lawn outside the visitors' entrance to the Castle. On Saturday nights, it is said, the two men can be heard at midnight, still playing cards and carousing and during the daytime, when school parties visit Glamis, children putting their ears to the wall maintain that they can still hear ghostly sounds echoing dimly through the time-honoured masonry.

Although it is debatable whether the Devil made a personal appearance at **Owlpen Manor**, it was devilish practices and dabbling in the dark arts that are thought to have brought into being the most unpleasant of this ancient house's hauntings. 'The alchemist', as Lady Mander refers

110

to the sinister presence, is in her words 'really nasty' – so nasty, in fact, that the room in the top of the house, reached by a spiral staircase, in which this sinister individual used to indulge in his nefarious studies, can no longer be used as a bedroom. Today it houses filing cabinets, papers and books. So many people have felt such a malevolent presence in this part of the house that formal exorcism seems the only solution to ridding Owlpen of its least desirable resident from beyond the grave.

The alchemist (some say wizard) is believed to be one of two former residents of Owlpen Manor. A possible candidate is the seventh Thomas Daunt, who was lord of the manor of Owlpen in Georgian times and the last of the Daunt line there. The other 'suspect' is a tutor to the family at some time in its distant past, who raised the Devil, wrote about sorcery and was found dead in his chair. Whoever he was, up in the attic floor, which his ghost stalks today, he is said to have immersed himself in black magic with such alarming results that his books and papers remained sealed up for a generation after his death. It was only in the 1830s that the vicar, Parson Cornwall, was summoned to destroy them in holy fire. A bonfire was built and as the sinister papers took light, awe-struck lookers-on saw black birds escaping from the flames and flying away.

Only a few miles across the Cotswolds from Owlpen, **Chavenage House** near Tetbury did in fact undergo an exorcism at the request of the grandmother of David Lowsley-Williams, who owns the fine Elizabethan house today. 'She did a belt and braces job,' her grandson remarks, 'by having a service performed jointly by both Church of England and Roman Catholic priests.' The room that required this formal religious attention was the bedroom in which Oliver Cromwell stayed when he visited Chavenage soon after the end of the Civil War, though before the execution of Charles I. As David Lowsley-Williams puts it, this room was always considered 'a bit nasty'. Nothing 'ghostly' was ever seen there; nothing was ever heard. But over the years guests sleeping there would awake during the night 'in a cold sweat, a real shivering funk – terrified, but not knowing why'.

With walls lined with dark patterned tapestries of great age, and heavy wooden furniture dark with the grime and polish of centuries, not to mention the wooden shutters that blank out much of the outside light even in the middle of the day, the appearance of Cromwell's bedroom alone could well unsettle guests.

After the exorcism, the malevolent atmosphere dispersed and there was 'very little trouble'. However, the atmosphere in that room has not cleared completely. During the filming of a BBC television drama, one of the actors playing a scene in Cromwell's bedroom suddenly went as white as a sheet, threw back the bedclothes and said, 'I'm sorry. I must get out and have a cup of coffee. I feel terrible and I can't remember any of my lines.'

Until her death in 1956, Princess Marie Louise of Schleswig-Holstein, who was one of Queen Victoria's granddaughters, was a regular visitor to Chavenage and in her memoirs she described a similar feeling passing the door to Cromwell's haunted bedroom:

111

To reach the staircase leading downstairs I had to cross the landing outside Cromwell's rooms. I am not a timid or nervous person by nature, but I am not ashamed to confess that I was honestly frightened to cross that landing – an odd feeling of something uncanny and horrid seemed to bar my way. Then I thought how I might protect myself and be rid of this terror. I made the Sign of the Cross, and after that I was no more frightened, and could run down the stairs happy and cheerful and free from that terrible feeling of oppression and evil.

Sleeping in other rooms at Chavenage has had a disturbing effect on people over the years. When the house was occupied by the military during the Second World War, an army chaplain and his wife were billeted there for a while, until the occasion when the chaplain had to go away for several days on duties elsewhere, leaving his wife in the house with David Lowsley-Williams's aunt, who was more or less running the house and sizeable farm with her mother. One morning, not long after the chaplain had left, the ladies of the house came down to breakfast to find a note written by his wife some time during the night. In it, the distraught woman had said that she couldn't take the ghostly atmosphere of the house any longer and was leaving Chavenage there and then to walk through the early hours to the railway station at Kemble, seven miles away.

It is unusual for men brought up in haunted houses to be affected by their supernatural forebears, but during the time that David Lowsley-Williams's son, George, slept in the room his father now uses as a dressing-room, he was often found in the morning buried deep in his bedclothes. It was only later, as an adult, that he explained he could sense something unpleasant in the room and felt safer if he was completely covered by his bedding. And he was not alone. Before David Lowsley-Williams inherited Chavenage from his uncle, that room had been used to accommodate guests, a fair number of whom would emerge in the morning complaining of not having slept well. They had been disturbed, they said, by an awful dream in which a man was leaning over their bed. In every case the description they gave of their nocturnal visitor was uncannily similar. He had long greasy black hair, a Mexican moustache and heavy gold epaulettes on his shoulders.

During the Second World War, Mr Lowsley-Williams's aunt took to sleeping in the room which had formerly been used by Colonel Nathaniel Stephens, Oliver Cromwell's friend who had owned Chavenage during the turbulent years of the mid-1600s. She started to feel her bed being nudged at night, as though someone had walked into it. This persisted to the extent that she decided to move her bed to another part of the room where the night-time knocks and bangs ceased right away.

Although her nephew is careful not to claim to have seen, or indeed experienced, anything 'ghostly' himself, there have been unexplained events at Chavenage when he has been present. On one occasion he was sitting in the main hall reading the paper, with his dogs lying around him 'toasting their tummies in front of the fire', when suddenly there was a low growling. All the dogs were sitting up, looking intently at the front door. As their master watched, their heads moved together as though their eyes were following some unseen visitor crossing through the hall. It could have been a rat under the floorboards, David Lowsley-Williams suggests. Based on the other sights and sounds at Chavenage House, however, it could well have been something else that troubled his dogs' keen senses.

During the 15th century, **Chenies Manor House** in Buckinghamshire played host on many occasions to two other notable figures in history: Elizabeth I and her father Henry VIII. It seems that Henry may well have returned to the house within the last fifty years, during the time when Mr and Mrs MacLeod-Matthews have owned the fine old house. Henry VIII paid at least one visit to Chenies during his brief and turbulent marriage to Katherine Howard: his flighty young wife who would soon lose her head after being found guilty of sexual impropriety. As a regular visitor, he no doubt knew the layout of Chenies well, knew too where lovers might meet in secret away from prying eyes. By this stage of his life the king was ageing badly. Bloated and in constant discomfort from a jousting wound that refused to heal, he

Chenies Manor House

walked with difficulty – but walk he may well have done around Chenies on that visit, dragging his swollen legs along passages and through outbuildings searching for Queen Katherine, hoping, perhaps, to catch her in the arms of her lover Thomas Culpepper.

That, at least, is the scene that came to the mind of Elizabeth MacLeod-Matthews on the night that she was woken from a deep sleep to hear heavy footsteps in the corridor at the top of the staircase outside her bedroom. Her husband was away and with the prospect of an intruder prowling the house, she dragged furniture in front of the two doors leading into the room and retreated to her bed while the sound of stomping echoed through the house. Her anxiety was mirrored in her Siamese cat which had been sleeping peacefully until she awoke. Now the poor creature was wide awake with its hair standing on end. That was before it fled underneath her bed and was violently sick.

At the same time Mrs MacLeod-Matthews was aware of the oppressive atmosphere in the room, 'so thick, it was as if you could cut it with a knife'. With no chance of going back to sleep in these conditions, she tried to take her mind off what was going on by reading *Country Life*. After an hour and a half, she realised that the atmosphere was beginning to lighten. The noise from the corridor outside her bedroom had faded away and dawn was approaching.

Later in the morning she mentioned what had happened to a keen historian who was researching the history of Chenies and asked her to check whether there was any significance about the date. Was there any record, she was interested to know, of Henry VIII and his entourage staying at Chenies on that date in September four centuries earlier? The answer was disappointing. Henry had been at Chenies during the month in question, but the dates did not tally – at least they did not tally until Elizabeth MacLeod-Matthews was going over what happened with her husband after he came home. It was he who pointed out that there had been a change in the calendar since Henry VIII's time. When this was taken into the calculation, the dates matched and the chances of his wife having heard the jealous old king ponderously exploring

Red Stairwell, Chenies Manor House

the house looking for his adulterous wife became more plausible.

That has been the only occasion when King Henry has disturbed the MacLeod-Matthews household quite so obviously. Interestingly, several visitors to the house have commented on feeling something peculiar at the same place in the house: the corridor at the top of the stairs and the very point where the sounds would have come from when they awoke the lady of the house. Her children too, like children in a good many haunted houses, admitted when they were older that they had hated going to the bathroom at night when they were little, because of something scary in the passage they had to cross – the same passage where the old king's ghost had woken their mother that September night.

Apart from this, Elizabeth MacLeod-Matthews happily reports that the atmosphere at Chenies is otherwise cheerful and welcoming, reflecting no doubt the care and loving attention she and her husband have given to restoring the house during its time in their stewardship. The same goes for **Levens Hall**, which Susan Bagot describes as being a warm and friendly house, despite its rather formidable appearance at night. However, Levens too has an unsettling atmosphere in places. A ley line is said to run through one part affecting a small drawing room and a bedroom above. One otherwise very down-to-earth friend of the family has admitted to having moved out of the bedroom to sleep elsewhere because she didn't like the feel of the room, and cleaners working in that same bedroom admit to getting through their work in there as quickly as possible because they feel uncomfortable.

The south wing of Levens Halls, which dates from the end of the 17th century, has a very noisy top corridor – noisier than might be expected in a house that is more than 300 years old. The noises heard here sound very much like those of a poltergeist.

At various times in their childhood, the Bagot children have reported experiencing unexplained activities. Susan Bagot says that her daughter

Bedroom at Levens Hall

once heard what sounded like a woman laughing. Her son has seen the figure of a man walking down the corridor towards him. On another occasion he raced into his parents' bedroom at night after he had been frightened by the sight of an old woman in his own room. Mrs Bagot admits to having heard very strange sounds when she was bathing her children at bedtime. The bathroom they used lay halfway along the corridor and while the children were being bathed, scratching noises could be heard on the other side of the bathroom door. Thinking that one of the dogs wanted to join in the bath-time fun, she opened the door and found that the corridor was empty. However, the noises were heard on other nights and the Bagot family have become accustomed to them, accepting that Levens is their home and they just have to get used to that fact that it is 'a very noisy corridor', as Susan Bagot phlegmatically describes it.

Not too far from Levens Hall, at **Muncaster Castle**, the Frost-Pennington family have come to accept the ghosts in their home 'as part of the furniture', according to Peter Frost-Pennington – though that was not always the case. When his children were still young they and their parents

Muncaster Castle

were interviewed by a reporter from Radio Cumbria, who was making a programme about Muncaster Castle.

Were there ghosts in the Castle, the reporter asked?

The two older children, the boys aged about 11 or 12 at the time, nonchalantly dismissed the suggestion, but their bravado was undone by their younger sister, who piped up and announced, 'Oh yes there are. And you're scared of them! And you won't go to the toilet on your own because you're so frightened of them.'

There was no recovering from that and indeed all three children had been uneasy about going up to bed on their own when they were young. Muncaster is fortunate in having a good-humoured ghost in the form of Tom Skelton, who was employed at some stage in its history as the resident fool or jester. He was a contemporary of William Shakespeare and any acts of unexplained 'tomfoolery' that occur at Muncaster are laid at his door. The Castle's last fool may have died 400 years ago but his playful spirit is still active.

Unfortunately the poltergeist that has made its presence felt at **Duncombe Park**, at Helmsley in North Yorkshire, has made far more of a nuisance of itself than Tom Skelton does at Muncaster.

Duncombe Park is the family home of Lord and Lady Feversham and its is they, their family and visitors who have suffered the unwanted attentions of what Lord Feversham refers to as 'the beast in the attic'.

Inhabiting the top storey of the house, 'this character, from time to time, cuts up rough and makes a heck of a din,' he continues, 'as though throwing heavy oak wardrobes or coffins about.' Admittedly, 'things have quietened down considerably' after a Catholic priest intervened a few years ago, but the poltergeist has not been sent packing completely.

For the most part the noise occurs at night, when the house is asleep, and people are woken by an appalling racket coming from the attic. Lord Feversham has torn upstairs in a rage more than once to put a stop to it, but when he arrived there has never been any sign of disturbance; all the furniture has been in place and everything has been as it should be – 'everything as quiet as a mouse'.

Nevertheless, his sister-in-law was once forced to leave the house when whatever was in the attic persecuted her by hammering on the floor above her bedroom with what sounded like a sledgehammer. On one or two occasions the poltergeist has been active during the daytime. When a decorator was working in one of the rooms on the top storey, the radio he was listening to at the other end of the room kept switching programmes.

The Feversham children have rooms on the top floor and they have been visited by their unwanted house mate on occasions, when it has turned their lights on and off.

It was keeping lights on (or rather candles lit) that challenged the occupants of the mill house at **Iford Manor** in the late 1980s. Among a number of curious aspects of living there was that they were unable to keep three candles alight in the ground floor sitting room. For some time one, or even two candles, would remain lit, but a third would invariably go out. Even with a replacement candle placed in a different part of the room to escape any possible draught, the same thing happened: the third candle would go out. After a while the situation became even more acute and every candle in that room faltered and died away. Even the husband (a doctor), who had been sceptical about the idea until that point, had to admit that no candles could be persuaded to stay alight there.

The same room also experienced 'other bizarre events' according to the owner, Mrs Cartwright-Hignett. The first was when an old oil lamp standing on a shelf in the sitting room was found with its glass mantle split right around its circumference in a perfectly straight cut, without any sign that it had been moved from its original position. Although it is known that certain atmospheric conditions, such as thunderstorms, can crack old high-fired glass and porcelain, for that to have accounted for such a perfectly symmetrical break seems unlikely.

Within a couple of months of this strange discovery, something even odder happened in the drinks cupboard in the room. When the doctor's wife went to pick out a tin of orange juice, she found that this too had been neatly cut in half around its circumference, so that when she lifted it only the top half came up in her hand. The bottom half of the tin was still filled with juice right to the brim and could not have been moved without spilling some.

The juice from the top half poured out when it was picked up, although some had already seeped out.

Before she was married, Mrs Cartwright-Hignett lived in Iford Mill by herself for a dozen years. For a while following the death of the former owners of Iford Manor, their housekeeper occupied the basement flat at the Mill. Having no television of her own, she was in the habit of often joining Mrs Cartwright-Hignett upstairs to watch hers. At about nine o'clock one evening there was a loud crash. Alarmed that the housekeeper had had a terrible fall on the stairs below, Mrs Cartwright-Hignett rushed down to the basement, only to run into the housekeeper who was hurrying upstairs concerned that she had fallen down them herself. That was just one of the many strange thumps, thuds and bangs that echoed through Iford Mill, only a few of which could have been accounted for by logs afloat on the mill stream banging into the walls below the house.

Supernatural disturbances of this kind are bad enough when you have to cope with them in your own home, but when the house is also the temporary home of other people, the problem is infinitely worse. This was the dilemma that Peter de Sausmarez faced only a few years ago at **Sausmarez Manor**. Part of the house had been converted into holiday flats and in the second year of letting them he was fortunate enough to find a lady artist who wanted to lease one of the flats during the winter, thereby ensuring some welcome additional revenue and allowing the central heating to be put on regularly. On the downside the tenant's arrival pretty much coincided with the beginning of extraordinarily loud and persistent noises – in no way connected with the tenant, but a cause of considerable concern for her landlord in case they frightened her away and brought her tenancy to an untimely halt.

The noises began as murmurings that seemed to come from a room adjacent to one in which Peter, his secretary or his partner happened to be. These gradually became louder and were joined by the sound of footsteps pacing about. Peter's secretary became increasingly unsettled by these noises and had started murmurings of her own that she would have to leave her job if things continued as they were. For her the final straw came the morning that she and Peter were working in his office when his partner, who was uncharacteristically ill, rose from her sick bed and stormed downstairs to berate him for having stomped about outside her bedroom and shouted at her through the door so inconsiderately. Both he and his secretary were nonplussed as neither of them had been out of the office since getting down to work.

That was enough for the secretary, who gave in her notice on the spot; but it didn't offer a solution to the mysterious noises in the house. That came from the unlikely source of a friend of the Dalai Lama. After Peter's partner explained the problem to this friend, she offered to have a word with a Tibetan monk she knew, whom she was sure would know what to do.

Ten minutes later she was back on the phone with clear, if somewhat peculiar instructions on how to exorcise the spirits. Onto a meat dish they placed dried sage leaves, which they then set alight to produce what amounted to a form of incense. Bearing this in front of him, Peter led the way through Sausmarez Manor chanting Tibetan mantras that had been dictated down the telephone line. Passing from room to room they made their way up to the top of the house, where the inevitable happened. As the ceilings got lower and lower, and the smoke proliferated, it triggered one of the smoke detectors and set the alarms ringing all over the house.

Putting down his smoking meat dish, Peter dashed downstairs to turn off the alarm to be met by his tenant who had followed correct procedure and was standing in what was designated as the assembly position in the event of fire.

Persuaded by her landlord that it was only a technical hitch, she returned to her flat to carry on with her painting. But when the alarm sounded again, she wasn't so easily dismissed. 'Are you sure it's only something technical?' she asked pointedly. 'Because I can smell some very funny smoke around here.'

It was only when she came to leave some months later that Peter de Sausmarez felt able to explain what had really been going on.

'Oh, you shouldn't have worried about that,' she replied. 'I've known about that all along, because I can definitely feel a friendly spirit in the house!'

Prior to this particular intruder, Peter de Sausmarez had to cope with something similar in the barn behind the house. When he first moved into the manor it was quite common to see an ethereal, bluish tinted, light shining at night from the gable of the barn. The building was unoccupied at the time and no amount of speculation or theory from guests and family could explain what was causing it. Apart from

The barn at Sausmarez Manor

anything else, as far as Peter knew the gable was solid masonry, covered by an extensive rambler rose. It was only after this rose had died and been cut back that the outline of a blocked-up window was revealed. Could the light have been a ghostly 'memory' of a time when lights had been lit inside the building? Who can say?

The light disappeared from the barn when the ground floor was converted into a tearoom. Some time later the upper floor was turned into a doll's house museum and after several months as tenants, each of those who has run the business has asked Peter de Sausmarez whether the barn is haunted by any chance.

When asked why, they have explained that on several occasions they have arrived in the morning to open up for business and have heard footsteps coming from the floor above. The first idea that crossed their minds, of course, was that someone had sneaked in without paying. On investigation, however, the doll's house museum upstairs has always been completely deserted.

'I can only assume,' says Peter de Sausmarez, 'that whatever was larking about with the blue light is still larking about upstairs in the barn.'

It was preventing light escaping from a window as part of the wartime blackout regulations that led to a very strange experience at **Powderham Castle**, near Exeter, for the late Lady Devon, mother of the current Earl of Devon, and Mademoiselle Cohard, his sister's governess. At the beginning of the Second World War they were hanging blackout material in the Castle in the course of which they came to a window on a landing at one corner of the house. Removing some boxes of shells from the windowsill, they each closed a shutter before checking from the garden that no light was visible. Satisfied that all was well, they continued with their work.

When Lady Devon went to close the shutters the following night, however, she was amazed to find that they she could not move them; both shutters were screwed back against the wall. She sent for Arthur Hitchcock, the house-carpenter, and asked him if he could account for what had

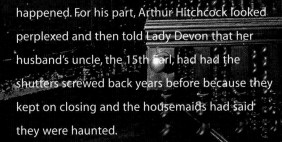

Powderham Castle

happened. For his part, Arthur Hitchcock looked perplexed and then told Lady Devon that her husband's uncle, the 15th Earl, had had the shutters screwed back years before because they kept on closing and the housemaids had said they were haunted.

Now it was Lady Devon's turn to look perplexed. With Mademoiselle Cohard as a witness, she insisted that they had closed them the previous evening. But when the house-carpenter pointed to the rusted screw heads, which had not been touched for years, and to the blind, that would

125

also have prevented the shutters being closed, it was clear that something very odd had happened. Both Lady Devon and the French governess were certain that they had closed both shutters and lowered the bar that kept them shut. Furthermore, the boxes of shells were still lying where they had moved them. Whatever had happened in that 24-hour period remains unexplained to this day.

This landing has also been the site of other strange events. On one occasion one of the family dogs refused to go though the doorway from the landing into the Lobby and ran up and down looking for another way to go. When it finally plucked up courage to pass through the doorway, it took a leap – jumping over something that no human present could either see or sense.

In very recent times, when photographs were being taken to illustrate the current visitor guide to Powderham Castle, the Haunted Landing was the only place in the house where the photographer encountered problems with his lights.

Any spectral manifestation can be disturbing, but when sounds, a sense of unease, or an unpleasant atmosphere send the pulse racing and make the hairs stand on the back of your neck, those can be the times when a disbelief in ghosts may need some reappraisal.

Returning to Owlpen Manor, Gloucestershire's most haunted house, Sir Nicholas Mander is eloquent in proffering one explanation of what may have happened in his home and other historic houses. If 'scratching a piece of plastic' can perfectly record the works of Mozart, he suggests, why should not people believe that 'stones can receive all the voices that have echoed in a room, storing them somehow in the walls for those sensitive enough to hear them'?

As ordinary mortals, he continues, most of us are only able to pick up a fleeting sense of what has been stored away in historic buildings. The fact that 'ordinary mortals' can be so profoundly affected by what they encounter points to the power and volume of what lies waiting for those able to tune in with far greater perception and understanding at Owlpen and every other 'haunted' building.

Gazetteer

Ballindalloch Castle
Banffshire, Scotland AB37 9AX
T: 01807 500 205
www.ballindallochcastle.co.uk

Beaulieu
Beaulieu, Brockenhurst
Hampshire SO42 7ZN
T: 01590 612345
www.beaulieu.co.uk

Bramall Hall
Bramhall Park, Bramhall
Stockport, Cheshire SK7 3NX
T: 0845 8330974
www.bramallhall.org.uk

Burton Agnes Hall
Driffield, East Yorkshire
YO25 4NB
T: 01262 490324
www.burton-agnes.co.uk

Chavenage House
Tetbury
Gloucestershire GL8 8XP
T: 01666 502329
www.chavenage.com

Chenies Manor House
Chenies, Buckinghamshire WD3 6ER
T: 01494 762888
www.cheniesmanorhouse.co.uk

Chillingham Castle
Chillingham, Alnwick
Northumberland NE66 5NJ
T: 01668 215359
www.chillingham-castle.com

Duncombe Park
Helmsley, York
North Yorkshire YO62 5EB
T: 01439 770213
www.duncombepark.com

Dunvegan Castle
Dunvegan, Isle of Skye
Scotland IV55 8WF
T: 01470 521206
www.dunvegancastle.com

Eyam Hall
Eyam, Hope Valley
Derbyshire S32 5QW
T: 01433 631976
www.eyamhall.com

Glamis Castle
Glamis, Angus
Scotland DD8 1RJ
T: 01307 840393
www.glamis-castle.co.uk

Iford Manor
Bradford on Avon
Wiltshire BA15 2BA
T: 01225 863146
www.ifordmanor.co.uk

Isel Hall
Cockermouth
Cumbria, CA13 0QG
T: 01900 821778

Kiplin Hall
Nr Scorton, Richmond
North Yorkshire DL10 6AT
T: 01748 818178
www.kiplinhall.co.uk

Knebworth House
Estate Office, Knebworth House,
Knebworth, Hertfordshire SG3 6PY
T: 01438 812661
www.knebworthhouse.com

Knowsley Hall
Prescot, Merseyside L34 4AG
T: 0151 489 4827
www.knowsley.com

Levens Hall
Kendal, Cumbria LA8 0PD
T: 015395 60321
www.levenshall.co.uk

Longleat House
The Estate Office
Longleat, Warminster
Wiltshire BA12 7NW
T: 01985 844400
www.longleat.co.uk

Muncaster Castle
Ravenglass
Cumbria CA18 1RQ
T: 01229 717614
www.muncaster.co.uk

Owlpen Manor
Near Uley
Gloucestershire GL11 5BZ
T: 01453 860261
www.owlpen.com

Powderham Castle
Kenton, Exeter
Devon EX6 8JQ
T: 01626 890243
www.powderham.co.uk

Prideaux Place
Padstow, Cornwall PL28 8RP
T: 01841 532411
www.prideauxplace.co.uk

Ripley Castle
Harrogate
North Yorkshire HG3 3AY
T: 01423 770152
www.ripleycastle.co.uk

Samlesbury Hall
Preston New Rd, Samlesbury
Preston PR5 0UP
T: 01254 812010
www.samlesburyhall.co.uk

Sausmarez Manor
Sausmarez Road
St Martin, Guernsey
Channel Islands GY4 6SG
T: 01481 235571
www.sausmarezmanor.co.uk

Tissington Hall
Ashbourne
Derbyshire DE6 1RA
T: 01335 352200
www.tissington-hall.com

Traquair House
Innerleithen, Peeblesshire
Scotland EH44 6PW
T: 01896 830323
www.traquair.co.uk

Whitmore Hall
Whitmore, Newcastle under Lyme
Staffordshire ST5 5HW
T: 01782 680478

Woburn Abbey
Woburn
Bedfordshire MK17 9WA
T: 01525 290333
www.discoverwoburn.co.uk

For further details on these
houses and other Historic Houses
Association members, please visit
www.hha.org.uk